Recovering the Margins of American Religious History

I0886184

RELIGION AND AMERICAN CULTURE

Series Editors

David Edwin Harrell Jr.
Wayne Flynt
Edith L. Blumhofer

Recovering the Margins of American Religious History

The Legacy of David Edwin Harrell Jr.

EDITED BY
B. Dwain Waldrep and Scott Billingsley

FOREWORD BY
Wayne Flynt

THE UNIVERSITY OF ALABAMA PRESS
Tuscaloosa

Copyright © 2012
The University of Alabama Press
Tuscaloosa, Alabama 35487-0380
All rights reserved
Manufactured in the United States of America

Typeface: ACaslon
Cover design by Gary Gore
∞
The paper on which this book is printed meets the minimum requirements of American National Standard for Information Sciences—Permanence of Paper for Printed Library Materials, ANSI Z39.48-1984.

Library of Congress Cataloging-in-Publication Data

Recovering the margins of American religious history : the legacy of David Edwin Harrell, Jr. / edited by B. Dwain Waldrep and Scott Billingsley.
p. cm. — (Religion and american culture)
Includes bibliographical references.
ISBN 978-0-8173-5708-5 (pbk. : alk. paper) — ISBN 978-0-8173-8609-2 (electronic) 1. Harrell, David Edwin. 2. Churches of Christ—History. 3. Protestant churches—United States—History. I. Waldrep, B. Dwain. II. Billingsley, Scott, 1968–
BX7077.Z8H37 2012
286.6092—dc23

2011042573

Contents

Foreword

David Edwin Harrell Jr.: Restoration Activist, Christian Globalist, Social Historian, Rigorous Mentor

Growing up Christian in the mid-twentieth century South—amid the first stirrings of neofundamentalism; the waning days of the social gospel movement; diminishing anti-Catholic, anti-Jewish Protestant sectarianism; and the glacial receding of religious sectionalism—produced some exceptional religious biographies. David Edwin Harrell's is one of them.

Born into a family of privilege—his father was a well-regarded physician in Jacksonville, Florida, and the family owned substantial land in southern Georgia—he and his siblings came of age awkwardly straddling Jacksonville's social elite and its religious fringe. Although by profession, wealth, and education they belonged to the city's upper crust, their membership in the Church of Christ branded them as quirky newcomers. Even worse were their poorer, pentecostal south Georgia relatives. That this seemed to bother the Harrells not at all may be the first clue to Ed's identity.

Not that the Church of Christ was all that doctrinally strange, socially unfamiliar, or economically marginal by the 1940s and 1950s. In fact, restorationist theology was beginning to receive the serious theological attention that the Stone-Campbell movement deserved. And wartime prosperity, coupled with rural to urban migration, had brought the dreaded "Campbellites" (as we newly mainstream southern Baptists preferred to disparage them) to a neighborhood near us all. Still, much of the tension born in social and class differences remained, and in some ways those two postwar decades were more like the first years of the twentieth century than they were like the 1960s.

I well remember my own dramatic conversion as a preteen in a downtown Birmingham church sometime around 1948 or 1949. The spiritual euphoria of the moment and my subsequent baptism by total immersion in the authorized New Testament way (the sense of personal guilt, the cry for forgiveness, the necessity for personal conversion, and the mode of baptism were all elements that Baptists shared with their restorationist brothers and sisters) were almost immediately diminished by an insensitive admonition to my proud parents by my Church of Christ minister/ relative: "It's wonderful that Wayne has made his profession of faith and been baptized," he volunteered without any request for comment from my parents, "but of course he is going to hell anyway."

Restorationist theology and my uncle's unrelenting pressure finally and reluctantly won the adherence of my sharecropper grandmother and grandfather, who left the Baptist fold for the Church of Christ. But the incident did not endear my uncle to me or to my parents.

To imagine such an unkind remark from Ed Harrell (who is probably significantly more conservative about church polity and theology than my relative), even if he actually believed it, is impossible. This urbane, sophisticated scholar—comfortably at home in the most rarified intellectual company, using the rationalism that so productively informs his scholarship also to confound his "liberal" enemies in the Church of Christ—inhabits quite a different religious cosmos.

Not that Ed is incapable of stiff-necked confrontations about any number of matters both religious and secular. In the Stone-Campbell tradition, he loves a good fight. He also profits from the knowledge common to every hayseed, redneck, provincial, rustic, and marginalized southerner throughout time: their enemies almost always underestimate them, which is their chief advantage. Their antagonists fall into the trap of mobilizing their arguments around stereotypes, personal opinion, and a series of half-understood "facts" borrowed from intellectuals who often let their preferences and prejudices substitute for primary research and rigorous analysis. During the decade-and-a-half we shared an office suite at Auburn University, not to mention at a variety of high octane intellectual conferences, conventions, and faculty seminars, I observed Ed demolish with stiletto-like precision (and obvious relish) many fatuous and largely vapid challenges to his fine mind.

Of course, a good mind and a fine education are primary assets. These Ed acquired over time (adolescent immaturity, startling good looks, athletic prowess, and a concurrent penchant for preconversion hell-raising made his acquisition a bit slower than mine, a subject better left to speculation). Once acquired, though, he mobilized these gifts in the same single-minded way for the study of American religion as for intramural restorationist religious debates. Whereas most of my scholarly friends and I meandered from one academic interest to another, Ed has moved not one degree from his early religious and historical enthusiasms. Religious historian he began. Religious historian he is. Religious historian he will always be. If there is a book on American religion he has not read, reviewed, or at least sampled, written during the past century, I can't imagine what it could be. Yet his knowledge of the history both of America and the developing world allows him to integrate this religious knowledge into a vast worldwide panorama.

Indeed, one of Ed's greatest contributions to scholarship is how his career has expanded beyond the boundaries of uniquely American religious phenomena. Just as the great twentieth-century historian C. Vann Woodward began his career writing the history of an obscure Georgia populist politician, then enlarged that study into a convincing socioeconomic analysis of the South, and ended with insightful studies about comparative history, Ed manipulated the collective biographies of a group of long-neglected backwoods pentecostals into a compelling portrait of America's religious underclass, a new kind of national history textbook integrating religion into the mainstream narrative, and an exciting comparative study of the healing, charismatic movements in the developing world. In an academic setting where the latest buzz words are *Atlantic migration* and *globalization,* Ed has for four decades lived in, lectured about, and frequently traveled to India where for two years he also headed the American Studies Research Centre in Hyderabad, the largest of many such government centers of cultural interchange. In India he competently explained America while respectfully learning about Asia and the Middle East. There also he discovered the expansive tentacles of pentecostalism, extending far from their home base in rural America into the ranks of the aspiring masses of Asia, Africa, and Latin America. Long before most scholars used the term *globalism,* Ed was already studying the incredible phenomenon of an Indian evangelist who drew audiences of more than one hundred thousand people to his mass healing rallies across India. That America could export pentecostalism as successfully as it had jazz and McDonald's seemed a surprising revelation to his colleagues. But to Ed this was only another manifestation of the way upwardly mobile lower classes worldwide find meaning in (rather than thoughtless, apelike mimicking of) American values, however much local practitioners may modify those values. Like enigmatic Mississippi novelists William Faulkner and Eudora Welty, Ed found in the local, provincial, and ordinary world of the rural and small town South, universal truths about the soul-hunger and material ambitions of the poor and aspiring masses everywhere. If Ed did not write history entirely from the bottom up, he certainly wrote it from the outside in. Beginning in those seemingly innocent (though we now know seminally chaotic) years of the 1950s, Ed became a pioneer, first of religion on the margins, then of people on the margins. Like his deeply felt (and carefully cultivated) image of himself as a loner, an outsider, a scholar beyond the magic circle of the social, religious, political, and intellectual consensus, he was drawn to people whose story mirrored his own.

To spend one's career explaining fundamentalists, Biblical literalists, pentecostals, faith healers, anti-institutional restorationists, and charismatic revivalists is one thing. To choose to do so from the platform of major secular research universities rather than from the church pulpit or respectable denominational college is something else again. Ed could have had his pick of the juiciest plums of restorationist-endowed chairs, college presidencies, or denominational posts. That he chose instead to spend his career at the universities of Georgia and Arkansas, at the University of Alabama at Birmingham and Auburn, probably tells us something about the man and the scholar: that even his choice of teaching venue was an attempt to bring to the people he wrote about what they most desired—respectability; that to be one of them, he had to become different from them; that to assist those one most cares about, one must sometimes establish credibility through self-criticism and separation.

Ed's understanding of himself as a social historian of American religion was no accident. He found intellectual history too abstract, too intellectually fuzzy, insufficiently objective and rational. Church history struck him as neither contextually sufficiently broad nor analytically rigorous enough. At the core of all religious institutions, he believes, lies the nexus of class, gender, and race. Many academics who share his theoretical construction substitute a politically correct pabulum for a fierce, unblinking exploration of social dynamics. After all, it is not only the predominant folk culture that shapes religious beliefs to its needs and mythology. An equally flawed subculture—liberal academic subjectivism—grounds its criticism of folk religion in a competing set of needs and mythology. Because Ed subjects institutions he loves and believes in to the same scrutiny as the ones he thinks flawed and which he rejects, most scholars end up more puzzled by Harrell than opposed to him.

Even more confounding to the academy is his fiercely held personal faith that is so out of keeping with his academic objectivism. Those who insist on the harmonizing patterns of yin and yang would do well to skip Professor Harrell altogether. On matters of personal faith, he is drawn to rationalism and Biblical authority and away from the relativism of gender, race, and class. On matters of scholarly research, he is drawn to religious people on the social and economic margins. He is an unabashed populist and a patriotic nationalist. He sides with the underdog in America and in the world, even when his underdog is a pentecostal whose theology he rejects; an anti-institutional restorationist like himself; a healing charismatic he believes to be a charlatan; or a westernized Moslem intellectual who longs for a world order that is neither Islamist, totalitarian, nor corrupted by western materialism. He was, as my departed father used to say, willing to fight a circle saw on behalf of a cause or person who needs a champion or deserves a hearing.

His pugilistic spirit could be lethal toward academic peers or graduate students who substituted opinions for information and personal preference for thoughtful analysis. He does not suffer fools gladly. In my decade-and-a-half academic residence next door to him at Auburn, I inadvertently overheard many conversations with graduate students who had come to the university specifically to work under this tutelage. No one was more encouraging in the presence of industriousness, intellectual discipline, and hard work. Ideological agreement counted for nothing to Ed. Intellectual rigor, prodigious effort, exhaustive research, and careful analysis meant everything. For students who shared Ed's deep personal faith or his sometimes-esoteric (at least, to me) restorationist doctrinal system and mistook such acquiescence for a kind of religious convergence that bestowed a benediction on their sloppy scholarship, there was always a stormy, teeth-grinding moment of truth. I came to appreciate the tough love he administered in very large doses: lifelong support and encouragement in return for maximum effort, withering criticism for laziness and foolish obstinacy. When I finally understood the full meaning of those exchanges next door, I had a new appreciation for the fierce restorationist debates he had so brilliantly explained in his books. If something matters enough for a person to fight about it, why give an inch to an opponent who gets it wrong, whether the "it" is an institutional Church of Christ editor or an obstreperous but obviously wrongheaded graduate student? For those who measured up to his standards but disagreed with his conclusions, there was never a better friend. For those who agreed with his conclusions but sought thereby mainly to curry his favor, he proffered neither respect nor support. For uneducated people who were both sincere in their convictions and faithful in their proclamation, he offered charitable understanding and genuine affection. For politically correct academics who refused to subject their own beliefs to the same rigorous scrutiny they expected from others, he expressed scorn and ridicule.

Of the many ways we can measure a man, none is more important than the breadth and variety of people who like him. Usually his family, friends, and those who agree with his opinions think him perceptive, insightful, and clever. It is a measure of Ed Harrell's stature as an American intellectual that those who do not know him, who are ignorant of nearly all the things this book reveals about him, as well as those who know him well and disagree vociferously with him, nonetheless like and respect him and have been enormously enriched by his scholarship.

Wayne Flynt
Distinguished University Professor Emeritus
Auburn University

Preface

When the editors of this volume of essays honoring David Edwin Harrell asked me to provide a preface, I felt honored and readily agreed. What could be easier? Summarize the book's chapters, reflect on my own reading of his work, toss in a few stories from thirty years of sipping coffee with him at "the meetings," and ship it off. As it turned out, however, that assumption proved as flawed as my supposition that the responsibilities of child rearing would end when the kids left for college.

Writing the preface posed three challenges. The first was finding an angle of vision that accommodated the sheer immensity of Harrell's literary output. I found that it was like trying to view Mount Rushmore. It required both looking down from thirty thousand feet up and then looking up from a spot on the ground that somehow disclosed the essence of the whole. Looking down, I saw landmark studies of the restorationist tradition, the pentecostal tradition, the southern black and white sectarian tradition, the entire United States in the twentieth century, the charismatic giants Oral Roberts and Pat Robertson, and a steady stream of occasional pieces on faith and history. If someone blocked out a week just to count the pages, the sum likely would eclipse that of any other historian of American religion (except perhaps for Martin Marty and Mark Noll). For the ground-level glimpse, one could do no better than to consider the opening line of Harrell's first book and quoted in Sam Hill's essay in this volume: "From the banking houses of New York to the steel mills of Pittsburgh, the cotton fields of Alabama, the gold fields of California—nineteenth-century America was a titan in adolescence." In one telling sentence, Harrell prefigured the breadth of his historical vision, his lifelong focus on the particularities of geographic place, his awareness of the power of the economic and social forces that shape human life, and his mastery of the rhythms of the English language. In that memorable passage, Harrell also intimated what the rest of that book and many subsequent works would argue: that people drew enduring religious meaning from the gritty realities of everyday life.

The preface posed a second challenge. How does one capture the legacy of Harrell's contribution to historical method? This statement represents no small irony since he rarely talked about method and, indeed, seemed to pride himself on possessing none to speak of. But he did. In one sense Harrell's approach might be summarized as simply trying to tell the truth about the past in three symphonic strokes. What happened? How did it happen? And why did it happen? Yet this simplicity concealed remarkable subtlety. Harrell's method began with prodigious and sedulous research in the primary materials. By prodigious I mean the systematic reading of "ephemeral" data—manuscript and printed documents typically written by people known to God but lost to history, not archived in university libraries, and preserved in hard-to-find leaflets and yellowed newspapers. By sedulous, I mean that he read it all, or at least seemed to. Reviewers, including me, have challenged Harrell on one point or another, but never, as far as I know, on the grounds that he overlooked, let alone suppressed, sources. Harrell not only read those texts but also collected and bequeathed them to other researchers, launching new lines of inquiry and inviting other historians to retrace his steps in the hope of expanding and enriching the conversation.

Harrell's method also entailed evenhandedness, objectivity, and a sense of priority. Evenhandedness meant narrating both the good and the bad. Telling the good about people, especially "redneck" white southerners the mainline academy found distasteful because of their class or their politics, took courage. Telling the bad about people, especially religious leaders whom churches liked to set on a pedestal, took even more courage. Objectivity meant an unflinching conviction that it was possible to read the primary materials, practically if not perfectly, unfettered by interpretive bias, and then to render them with an unerring ear for the cadences of daily speech. James Goff's essay allows that at least one distinguished reviewer found Harrell's epistemic assumptions flawed. Yet given Harrell's suppositions, born in the bright sunshine of Enlightened Commonsense Realism, he established a gold standard for historical truth telling. And Harrell's sense of priority meant knowing the difference between things interesting and things important. He resolutely shunned the former and sought the latter. Things interesting featured local color stories and eccentrics on display. Things important featured the forces that truly mattered, and, in Harrell's view, those were less theological than social. Although his mind contained not a hint of political correctness, he pioneered concepts of race, class, and gender long before most secular historians, not to mention most church historians, came to terms with those powerful challenges to academic complacency. And though he was not a Marxist, at least not in any systematically theorized way, his work left little doubt that hard times, cultural marginalization, and the perennial human longing for simple respect drove the wheels of religious movements.

The preface's third and most difficult challenge lay in finding some way adequately to convey the power of Ed's personal example. (Here I switch to the name by which his countless friends have known him.) Explicitly or implicitly all of the essays in this volume eventually come around this point. The course of Ed's life readily divides into three parts. The first, for lack of a better term, might be called deportment. It is hard to decide which aspect of Ed's presence I most remember: his dapper wardrobe, his golfing prowess, his ready laugh, his self-deprecating wit, or his dinner table conviviality. Exactly why the Lord chose to bestow so many endearing traits on one person remains a mystery, but I am glad he did.

The second part of Ed's personal example was, as Wayne Flynt's essay suggests, a carefully cultivated outsider posture in the historical guild. This is not to suggest that the posture was disingenuous; indeed, Ed held it intensely and authentically. But it does suggest that he disdained the unself-critical pretensions of the academic elite. To be sure, he played by the rules of the profession. All data, warrants, and conclusions remained open to rigorous public critique. But inhabiting the profession's world did not mean inhabiting its universe. Everything Ed wrote seemed to say that when the rapture comes, the folks with calluses on their hands will go up first.

And finally there was Ed's Christian faith, the faith of a lifelong member of the so-called anti-institutional wing of the Churches (or churches) of Christ. Ed was no ecumenist. Both Richard Hughes's and Beth Schweiger's essays offer evidence that he felt that those who read the Bible substantially differently were not only wrong, but culpably so, and therefore lost. That Ed *really* believed that, I doubt. Or if he did, he gave no hint of it in how he treated Methodist outlanders like me, a treatment marked by unfailing generosity of spirit. I think, rather, that such statements represented Ed's slightly flamboyant yet deadly earnest way of saying that matters of faith were not trivial, and that men and women dithered at their eternal peril.

The splendid essays in this volume also fall into three parts. In part I, Samuel S. Hill, James R. Goff Jr., Richard T. Hughes, and Charles Reagan Wilson reflect on Harrell's contribution to, respectively, American religious history, pentecostal history, restorationist history, and southern history. In part II, Scott Billingsley, John C. Hardin, and B. Dwain Waldrep—all (like Goff) former Harrell students—offer expertly crafted studies of the "underside" of southern religious history. Their work reveals Harrell's masterful mentoring skills in action. Finally, in the introductory and the concluding essays, Wayne Flynt and Beth Barton Schweiger ruminate, respectively, on how the academic and the nonacademic sides of Harrell's life influenced each other. In different ways, they suggest that the influence was so strong the distinction makes little sense to begin with. Taken together, these essays offer a roadmap to the mind, if not the "authorial heartbeat" (as Sam Hill nicely puts it) of one of the most productive, influential, and gifted historians of modern times. That he also ranked as an unfailing encourager and dear friend of a legion of slightly younger academics like me may not earn him a permanent spot in heaven, but I am certain that it will earn him a permanent tee time on the celestial links.

Grant Wacker
Professor of Christian History
Duke University

Acknowledgments

The editors would like to thank, first and foremost, the subject of this volume. Ed Harrell has inspired many young scholars to pursue a career in history and explore the margins of mainstream American religion; he has challenged a few older scholars to sharpen their interpretations of America's story in light of his insight into restorationism, pentecostalism, and fundamentalism; and he has encouraged us all to not overlook what he has called the "underside" of American religion. Without his scholarship and mentoring, the field of American religious history would be less nuanced and would contain significant gaps in the story.

Several of the essays in this collection were presented at conferences, including meetings of the American Society of Church History and the American Academy of Religion. We are especially grateful to the editors of *Restoration Quarterly* for granting us permission to reprint Samuel S. Hill's essay, which originally appeared in that publication in 2004. We are also thankful for the contributors who so graciously agreed to write essays for this volume. They are not only giants in their respective fields of study, they are also supportive colleagues who have been a constant source of encouragement to the editors throughout this process. The staff at The University of Alabama Press has been very patient and has done a marvelous job of shepherding this project through to publication.

Finally, this book would not be possible without the financial support of the following individuals and institutions: Margaret Armbrester, Mrs. John R. Cook Sr., Wayne Flynt, John Hardin, Dr. James F. Tent, *Christianity Magazine,* Florida College, Harding University, Southeastern Bible College, and the University of North Carolina at Pembroke's Faculty Research and Development Grant. The editors are most grateful for the generosity these people and institutions have shown to us and to Ed in making this festschrift possible.

Recovering the Margins of American Religious History

PART I

1
David Edwin Harrell Jr.
American Religious Historian

Samuel S. Hill

"All history writing is autobiographical." Not quite, not exactly. But that statement, hardly indisputable truth, does lead us toward some insight into the dynamics of the historian's practice of his craft.

My respect for David Edwin Harrell Jr. is too great, and my sensitivity too genuine, I trust, for me to claim exhaustive knowledge of why he writes as he does. But I have both right and responsibility to ponder the outlines of his imagination. What is the Harrell appetite? What are the patterns of his reflection; what are his fascinations? Imagination, appetite, fascinations. My goal here is to put a stethoscope to the authorial heartbeat of this friend and colleague.

What is the range of the Harrell published corpus? In no particular order of significance, several categories loom, beginning with the history of his own brotherhood, the Churches of Christ. His first two books marked a turning point in the study of that movement and, I may say, in the young and growing, now massive, enterprise called American religious history. *Quest for a Christian America* and *Sources of Division in the Disciples of Christ, 1865–1900* were examinations of the tradition in hard-nosed historical fashion.[1] His most recent publication returns to that general theme but is a very different kind of book. *The Churches of Christ in the Twentieth Century: Homer Hailey's Personal Journey of Faith* is much more limited in scope and more focused in interest than Harrell's original historical studies.[2] And it seems that Harrell by now was so drawn to key figures, to shapers of religious currents, that he saw fit to let such a person help guide the reader through the story of the denomination's historical developments. It's worth noting that making one book of two studies registers editorial decisions by The University of Alabama Press, not a program of action that Harrell had firmly in mind or insisted on—notwithstanding his being one of three editors of the series published by Alabama that includes this book.

In *All Things Are Possible,* Harrell next explored the history of Spirit-driven, Protestant-concerted ministries and revivals from the end of World War II to 1974.[3] This book also ventured into territory that was largely foreign to mainstream historical scholarship. Not many scholars or readers gave much respect or attention to the healing revivals of a pretty motley crew of zealots—charlatans in the eyes of more than a few—who perpetrated these excitements and bromides on an unthinking, working-class public, as so many judged. As careful historian that he always intends to be and as listener to the stories of leaders and followers, Harrell explored two stages of this effervescence: the first, healing, modulating into a second, the charismatic. Not all gatherers of data on this general topic would so perceptively have seen the distinction between healers and charismatics, and certainly would not have had the wit to formulate the distinction as a modulation. Partly in consequence of his undeniable salesmanship capacities, a major house, the Indiana University Press, brought this book to the public, doing well for itself and encouraging scholarly interest for these "sectarian" causes.

Biographical studies comprise a third arena of Harrell's interest. Indiana University Press issued *Oral Roberts: An American Life* in 1985.[4] I am guessing that this achievement tops the list of the general readership's knowledge of Harrell's work. That supposition comes from several factors, of course, not least the exhaustive research represented by the six-hundred-page tome. Perhaps it was only bad luck that the next book, also a biography, did not push *Oral Roberts* to second position. What if Pat Robertson had been the Republican Party nominee for the presidency in 1988—and been elected to the highest office in the land? "What if" ruminations aside, Harrell published *Pat Robertson: A Personal, Religious, and Political Portrait* with Harper and Row in 1987.[5] Obviously, biography as a genre is in there somewhere, filling some corner of that vital Harrell imagination, impelling some of those appetites.

Sectarian phenomena are a fourth category prominent in Harrell's work. He has been at that since *White Sects and Black Men in the Recent South* appeared in 1971.[6] There he did some pioneering labor, or more accurately, saw some rarely recognized sights as his scrutinizing eye scanned the screen of Protestant life in parts of the southern highlands region near which he had lived as a professor at East Tennessee State University and at the University of Georgia. In the setting of the civil rights movement, it was easy to forget, also invigorating to note, that some of the most "backward" movements among pentecostals and holiness people had been putting into practice for several decades what the front-page efforts of the liberal religious establishment were aiming, at considerable cost, to make happen. Racial integration was, in fact, no great rarity among sectarian people, where black members sat beside white members; black and white testifiers gave God the glory with spirit and freedom of expression during the same church services. Women and men of European descent and African origin together glorified God without restraint and with boundless joy. I am not aware that Harrell's effort registered much impact, probably because in part the crusade to open the society was directed at the central public institutions and policies of the South and the nation. Never mind that intelligible strategy enacted by mainstream churches, the job didn't need doing throughout all of Dixie's congregations and denominations. Some of the churches had come upon that achievement without developing any strategy at all, just through responding to the divine spirit at work.

Harrell persisted with this theme in several essays published between 1981 and 1988. During the season when the enterprise of "southern religion" was gaining momentum and achieving identity, he was one of a small cadre of scholars regularly showing up at conferences and symposia, a company that included rather predictably John Boles, Wayne Flynt, Charles Wilson, Donald Mathews, and me, sometimes joined by such outlanders as Edwin Gaustad and Martin Marty. Each of us seemed to have a slot, Harrell's standard assignment being to tell us about regional sectarians who, even that late, were out of sight or beyond the range of serious examination. There is a Harrell glossary for the phenomena that consumed his attention; in addition to "sectarian," he wrote of the "underside" of regional religious life, minorities, nonconformists, and even "fanatics on the fringe." Treatment of bodies so described, of course, became the subjects of the first two Harrell books, his own people hailing from the southern, Stone-descended wing of the Stone-Campbell restoration movement. In that sense, "sectarian" phenomena deserve no truly special classification, being the subject of virtually all the religious groups he has studied. We need only to be sure to acknowledge that these sorts of Christian bodies were worth the scholar's time and that Harrell looked them over.

The year 1981 saw the publication of *Varieties of Southern Evangelical-*

ism.[7] Harrell was the editor of this collection of essays; indeed, The University of Alabama at Birmingham (UAB) symposium in 1979 that generated this body of work was very largely of his doing. It is a fine study and was an early airing of the broad range of religious constituencies in the South. The literature on denominations had long been with us, and historical and sociological interpretations of the interaction of church and society had been gaining a hearing. But here, driven by the Harrell predisposition to attend to the other 30 or 40 percent, we read about the social gospel of the South, black folk religion, Billy Graham, a breakdown of types of piety, and of course, Harrell's piece on the South as "seedbed of sectarianism." Some of the regulars appeared behind that UAB lectern, but so did Martin Marty, Joseph Washington from the University of Pennsylvania, and William Martin from Rice University. I repeat: that is a fine collection of essays, to this day one of the best composite studies of religion in the region. I remember admiring Harrell's willingness to use "Evangelicalism" as the blanket title term, since he deigned or decided to include the Churches of Christ, notably his branch off that trunk, under that title. Few observations that I have made in writing have been quoted more often than my "typology" of southern evangelicalism in an essay of that book. Harrell noted in his introduction that we learn in my contribution what Sam Hill likes and what he doesn't like, an *un-compliment* given with a grin and no dagger.

Clearly, Harrell's published work is extensive, has been carried on for more than four decades, and may be said to feature: Churches of Christ history, the historical tracing of special kinds of Spirit-infused movements, biography of religious leaders, and work on outside-the-mainstream sectarian bodies and perspectives. What do these lines of inquiry have in common? One historian has produced them all; the broad reaches of these investigations strike the reader of samples of each. The approach is always historical. Interpretation is present, certainly classification. But never—some demur over that absolute—does Harrell stray from the canons of his guild. He is a faithful, rather old-fashioned collector of data, recognizably a social historian, one who is dedicated resolutely to the documentation of what he presents. He is not a C. Vann Woodward sort of cultural historian, nor a member of the Dan Carter school of historiography. Harrell and Joel Williamson are very far apart indeed. He does not share Edwin Gaustad's love of ideas nor Martin Marty's passion to give everybody the benefit of the doubt and to bring everybody together. Conversations with Harrell disclose thoughtful reflection on meaning and reveal considerable wisdom. He listens with respect and responds with engaging interest. Yet he has been known to come down hard on scholars' expressions of opinion about or preference for particular points of view.

I mention two incidents in illustration of this point. Harrell tells me that when speaking to Muslims who are scholars of Islam, as he has done often in South Asia, he begins by telling them, straight out, that they are wrong, that Islam is misguided. Not just that he disagrees, but that they are wrong. From that point he "negotiates," in the sense of inviting dialogue, aiming thereby to achieve fairness that engages, listens, and goes somewhere. That tack elicits some respect from me, that is, the straightforward approach is legitimate and may well evoke elementally human interaction. This is a fine Harrell skill. But in this discussion of his historiography, the issue becomes Harrell's high standards of "getting it right," being accurate. Those who subscribe to false teachings are to be challenged.

This attitude is perfectly consistent with the philosophy of truth that Harrell spelled out in his 1966 Reed Lectures.[8] There he espoused Francis Bacon's doctrine of "double truth," the philosophical bifurcation of reality common in Enlightenment thinking most famously associated with Immanuel Kant. The Bacon affirmation summarizes as: "philosophy should be kept separate from theology." He readily acknowledges that this perspective is a kind of schizoid view of truth. In any case, revealed truth is knowable, knowable with the precision and infallibility that characterizes our knowledge of the natural world through science. There is truth and there is error, just as much in religious belief as in physics.

A second incident took place during a breakfast conversation at an annual meeting of the Southern Historical Association about 1982. I pulled out the old chestnut; let's compress our respective philosophies of life to one word. I said, "meaning"; he said, "obedience." You have just learned something about the speaker and the one whose work is being spoken about. Harrell, the self-characterized religious legalist, and the eminent scholar are the same person. That's a compliment, in the first instance, and in the second, it assists our understanding of his regarding "objectivity" as something attaining near-fetish proportions.

There is a lightness of being in Harrell as everyday father, husband, friend, and colleague that is not so evident in either his religious bearing or his scholarship. I confess to taking pleasure from reading his personal sketch in John Boles's book of autobiographical reflections by several southern religious historians.[9] Distinctions are drawn there that I had not seen in the normativist inclinations present in religious conversations or near the surface in his historiography. "Obedience," his one-word summary of "what makes him tick," transfers rather readily, it seems to this observer, to religious legalism and total dedication to objectivity in the practice of the historian's craft. Incidentally, I seem to have noticed that many biblical scholars from this tradition are more drawn to linguistic study than to theology, to examination of parts and pieces more than to broad themes or the whole. Please note that I celebrate the truth that it takes us to begin to deal adequately with the biblical material. The point I put forward is that there may be a similar mentality, in the form of an epistemology, linking such biblical scholarship and the kind of historical work that Harrell does. Perhaps even between Alexander Campbell's "gospel facts" and historical data.

The latest full-length book publication of course is *The Churches of Christ in the Twentieth Century: Homer Hailey's Personal Journey of Faith*, a study that has been greeted with general acclaim and some spirited opposition.[10] What has this book to do with the absence of lightness of being, to "obedience" writ large, as I have just ventured to interpret, in other words, to Harrell's high dedication to objectivity as historian? Honestly, this outsider to the Churches of Christ is far from certain. I am unable to decode the symbols of this brotherhood (and, by the way, of the Episcopal Church that I chose to join thirty-one years ago). One may have to be born to some system of symbolics in order to grasp them. But it is clear that some other professional historians judge that this book stacks the deck, is markedly unfair, indeed erroneous, falls short of the sought high standards. I raise this issue, not a pleasant one, because you are scholars within the brotherhood, and need to come face to face with who did what to whom in the twentieth century. Perhaps the book's second title, printed appositively to the first, namely, *Homer Hailey's Personal Journey of Faith*, has contributed to the sharp difference of interpretation.

Earlier I made reference to Harrell's addressing Islamic audiences in South Asia. To a greater degree than almost all scholars of my acquaintance, he has been involved in and given leadership to overseas cultures. Preoccupation with a person's publications may cause us to overlook other features of that scholar's career, contributions, and achievements. In the case of this scholar, the oversight is dramatic. From reading his curriculum vitae and from engaging him in conversation, I have become aware of his exceptional service to this country, to international affairs, and to interfaith understanding. I commend to you these facts: From 1993 to 1995 Harrell directed the American Studies Research Centre in Hyderabad,

India. Earlier he had been Senior Fulbright Scholar in Allahabad, India. Cutting short a long list of offices and honors, I mention these: selection as a distinguished USIA lecturer; a special ambassadorial citation from the US Ambassador to India; and membership on scholarship selection committees here and in India. He has lectured in India, Nigeria, Indonesia, Nepal, Bangladesh, Sri Lanka, China, and Egypt, also England and Australia. Harrell is a man of parts. Scholars do more than publish. This has been especially true of Harrell's career.

Possessing no powers of clairvoyance, I cannot predict what exactly from the Harrell corpus will last the longest, or will make the greatest positive contribution. But somewhere high on such a list will appear *Unto a Good Land,* an American history textbook published in 2005.[11] Largely Harrell's brainstorm, this is not just another such book intended for college classroom use. It is, rather, a serious resource for grasping American history that adds religious history to the conventional elements: the political, the military, the economic, the literary, the social/cultural, and so on.

Reading two of Harrell's chapters has left me with some impressions. First is the sheer skillfulness of his writing. We are at the moment spotlighting a marvelously gifted, much accomplished historian, something we have known all along. But I invite you to peruse bookend quotations. The first sentence of his first book, which began as his Vanderbilt dissertation, reads: "From the banking houses of New York to the steel mills of Pittsburgh, the cotton fields of Alabama, the gold fields of California—nineteenth-century America was a titan in adolescence."[12] Well, I could have locked myself in Descartes's Rotterdam garret for five days and not generated "a titan in adolescence." Now turn to a 1999 essay on Walter Scott—not the Scottish poet and novelist—and listen to the last sentence. "Walter Scott, like many of his generation of Americans, came to the factious and bellicose United States on the eve of secession and war bewildered and somber, an old man who had dreamed impossible dreams and seen misleading visions."[13] "Impossible dreams" here hardly carries the optimism of Don Quixote's aspirations.

Second, the weaving of religious developments in American life into the broader fabric is beautifully done. A pretty thoughtful reader could easily miss the incentive for producing this particular textbook (many didn't know we needed another one), namely, the inclusion of religious themes. Their inclusion is so deftly accomplished that, waked up, we might later ask how they could be left out. In the chapter on the Great Depression,

Harrell describes ideologies that were available to offer some constructive resources to the society during this tragic period. John Dewey is prominent, as are the social scientists with their analyses and nostrums for reclaiming life from the despairing existence afflicting so many millions. The inadequacies of social reform as promoted by liberal churches and their confreres bent on doing good are highlighted. The popular appeal of radio and print messages from those who would blame our ills on some scapegoat is given due attention. We learn of anti-Semitic diatribes, of latter-day nativism, of socialists and Marxists who peddled their solutions to this bankrupt nation. The early signs of the recrudescence and enlarged mission of conservative Protestant churches are shown. Neoorthodox theology gains a hearing. On these last two, it's a bit difficult to imagine traditional textbooks bothering to take note, perhaps with the exception of Reinhold Niebuhr's life. And on and on. Let me repeat: this study is a comprehensive and quite standard presentation of American history in the decade of the 1930s. The roles of organized religion and of spiritual searching and message promoting are simply woven in. How they could have been omitted, or their importance played down, becomes the issue for the discerning reader. There is nothing politically correct, or incorrect, or political at all, about the way the story is told in what should be a widely adopted resource for college underclass courses.

A second sample Harrell chapter bears the title, "A Turn to the Right: The Era of Reagan and Bush." Here the direct references to religion, broadly conceived, are fewer in number but by no means are reduced in influence. The so-called culture wars are given the play they deserve—and better, that designation discloses that "religion" in any usage is an inadequate title for doing justice to the ideological, attitudinal, and ethical dimensions of the society's life. All bound up together are patriotism, natural law theory, economic philosophy, the spread of democratic government across the world, moral absolutism, and the elevation of family and sexual issues to lofty priority. Ronald Reagan's implicit, not explicit (or confessional) incorporation of religious teachings into "traditional values" is featured. Pat Robertson, James Dobson, Jerry Falwell, and Jim and Tammy Bakker enjoy moments in the sun. In his picturing of the 1980s, just as in the Depression era, Harrell imperceptibly folds into the larger package religious-attitudinal-ethical-spiritual elements prominent in the national life at the time. Based on what I have read, I commend the vision and skill of authors and editors who have included something without making that something THE agenda.

What is the legacy of Harrell's career so far? How is he being influential? What sort of impact is he making on the study of American religious history? Several points of significance appear as we reflect on those questions. I judge it fair to conclude that there is no notable Harrell school of interpretation. His work is standard and conventional on that score. He is, indeed, a kind of old-fashioned collector of data. Over and over I am impressed with his prodigious research, with no slacking, from dissertation days to the present.

Ah, but in the area of biography, he has greatly transcended conventionality and has gone to the most industrious lengths to understand his subjects. Harrell's study of the life of Oral Roberts is a model deserving emulation by other scholars.[14] Just how many hours did the subject and author spend together? What price did he pay to gain Roberts's attention and win his confidence? That entrée did not come easily, we may be certain. Thus, "conventional" and "old-fashioned" do not equate with ordinary, certainly not with pedestrian. Most admirable of all is Harrell's identification with this faith-healing giant, with this larger-than-life entrepreneur of ventures as diverse as higher education, tent revivals, and television. Empathy abounds. We readers are left with assurance that confidences are being honored, that listening is occurring with the third ear, and that respecting the intentions of a complex, busy, often-condescended-to and controversial figure is an inviolable commitment of the biographer. The same qualities appear in Harrell's treatment of Pat Robertson's life, but that book is less effective, for several reasons that seem to be pretty apparent: first, the Robertson study had to be written in a hurry—the 1988 election was looming; and second, Robertson is less accessible to most academic/intellectual minds at work.[15] (We do not have much experience in analyzing someone extraordinary in the ways that Oral Roberts is.) But in both cases, the requisite work was done, fairness prevailed, and empathy was dished out in heavy, tasteful portions.

Harrell makes no particular contribution to theory. He does not work with a self-conscious reference to what, exactly, historiography is about. He does his work, as noted, in a kind of traditional way. I have wondered how his work might be treated in a history graduate seminar dealing with methodology. Nothing startling or particularly subtle or innovative exudes from his writings. One is apt to pay more attention to what he is doing than to how he is doing it. That is a mark of a skillful narrativist.

I conclude that the subjects he chooses define his work the most acutely. We have thus circled back to issues raised earlier. What is the Harrell appetite, what fascinates this particular historian, what are the contours of his imagination? "Narrative" seems to me to outline these contours. But narrative about what? "Sectarian religious movements" could be the answer. But that summary misleads as well as depicts.

Looking again at the list of publications, we find that a large portion treat the history of the Disciples of Christ/American restorationist tradition. The other dominant topic of attention is outside-the-mainstream religious movements and celebrity leaders within them. That sheaf includes the healing and charismatic revivals of the third quarter of the twentieth century and the emergence shortly thereafter of two nationally prominent figures, Oral and Pat, who, respectively, rose to the Big Time against heavy odds and took advantage of high-level connections and innate giftedness to move to national prominence.

What do we have here? I submit, an intriguing dyad of sensibilities, distinctive from but fetchingly related to the "double truth" theory from the thought of Francis Bacon that attracted Harrell early on. Do not let me get by with any cleverness that implodes upon its own deviousness. Does Harrell's understanding of religion—and maybe life itself—require comparative thinking? Edward Tylor wrote more than a century ago that it is necessary to understand two religions in order to understand one.[16]

Look at Harrell's topics of interest. One, the Stone-Campbell movement, pursues a definitively rationalist grasp of truth and perception, emphatically so in the case of his own anti-institutional wing of that tradition. The other roots in and trusts personal experience, what he refers to as subjectivist. Here we are again: objectivity and subjectivity. I judge that Harrell's typical outlining of the world of truth and persons regularly falls into this dual classification. There is scholarly analysis that is either valid because it is objective or invalid owing to its subjectivity. Likewise, there are two elemental religious universes of understanding. We know what his is, objective truth, made perfectly clear in those Reed Lectures of 1966; the other is the religion of the heart, of feelings, that is bound to trip one up.

There is no reason to suppose that Harrell labored over any need to defend the validity of his own universe of understanding by contrasting an erroneous alternative with it. The healers and charismatics, and most attractively Oral Roberts, are not setups chosen so as to reinforce his own convictions grounded in the epistemology by which he declares his own faith. Yet his curiosity about that other half is palpable. By the way, I never detect in his writing any condescension or judgmental spirit toward the subjectivists. They are not, so to speak, stuck in his craw. I have had occasion to wonder whether, probably unwittingly, Harrell is gentler with movements from the underclasses than with those from our society's "ruling classes." Those who ought to know better do seem to come in for some hard blows. That includes misguided restorationists, Muslims (fellow rationalists, by the way), and many who claim to follow the biblical teachings.

In passing, I mention that many Christians operate in a world of triads or multiplexes or mystery: Luther with nominalism, and incarnationists who affirm that the Divine Presence knows no epistemic limits, among them. In those settings, ambiguity and unbelief do not presuppose or imply each other. The method of thinking that Harrell embraces harbors no place for irony, for correlative understanding, or for dialectical reasoning.

Finally, on a different subject, we note that the Harrell legacy in historiography attends to the issue of American spatiality. Any glance at his publications gives hints that his work is bounded by the South, meaning Virginia to Texas and Oklahoma—in other words, the heartlands of the Churches of Christ and the Charismatic revival. But hints are not borne out by facts. The textbook chapters I have read reveal sophistication in general American history. That comes as no surprise, since Harrell has been teaching in that field for more than four decades at East Tennessee State, Georgia, Oklahoma, Arkansas, University of Alabama at Birmingham (twice), and Auburn. Moreover, his research on the Healing revivals showed him, and helped awaken us all to the interregional, truly national, character of that expression of modern American spirituality. To citizens in Milwaukee, Seattle, and Boston, the South may have seemed the natural birthplace of such strange behavior. But historical accuracy does not allow that interpretation. Neither fundamentalism nor holiness (in any form, really) is indigenous to the South. I had never before thought to thank Harrell for helping open up the boundary-defying force of spirit-led movements. His work in *White Sects and Black Men,* a parochial study, turns out to have pioneered his treatment of ubiquitous religion-of-the-heart "sects." What is really important is not so much any historian's alertness to this but the obliviousness of such sects to boundaries of any kind.

Simple courtesy suggests that I express in a public way that at several stages I have been aroused from my slumbers by Harrell's work; also that I thank my inviters for asking me to take on this assignment. I am grateful.

David Edwin Harrell Jr. might have been lots of things that he is not, if you take your cue from personal charm and good looks, from the most developed tastes in fine clothes of any academic colleague I know, and from excellence in golf and athletics generally. Harrell is a major historian who has greatly advanced the work of doing the history of the Stone-Campbell tradition, who also has helped open for the nation an understanding of once-ignored or condescended-to Christian movements, showing us what they are and how influential they are in the public life of this republic.

From my perspective, his most valuable contribution is as an embodiment of a total calling. Teacher, publishing scholar, internationalist, adviser to students and colleagues, one who makes things happen. I believe I recognize excellence when I see it—certainly, very clearly in him. Well done, "well doing," Ed. Carry on.

2
Elijah's Never-Failing Cruse of Oil
David Harrell and the Historiography of America's Pentecostals

James R. Goff Jr.

From my days as a graduate student at the University of Arkansas, I recall one Sunday afternoon when David Harrell and I attended a church dedication service in nearby Rogers, Arkansas, conducted by our mutual friend Vinson Synan. On the way back to campus, we discussed personal insight into our own religious traditions—for me the Pentecostal Holiness Church, for Harrell, the Church of Christ. At the time, I was still considering my own place and future within the pentecostal movement, and the one thing that stuck with me from that drive was Harrell, the mature scholar, sharing with me, his student and very much a "wannabee" scholar, his place in his own denomination. He said something to the effect, "In my denomination, I *am* kind of a minister; I consider myself a lay preacher of sorts." For me, at that age and at that time in my life, the comparison gave me a firm sense that I could endure and climb the mountain of controversy to find my own niche in the church while at the same time pursuing a career as a serious scholar. I appreciated his example much more than I suppose he knew. So, for an occasion like this, it is entirely appropriate to begin with a Bible verse: "And the barrel of meal wasted not, neither did the cruse of oil fail, according to the word of the LORD, which he spake by Elijah," I Kings 17:16 (KJV).

The Old Testament verse concludes the story of the prophet Elijah's encounter with a poor woman, a widow whose generosity to God's spokesman was rewarded with a miracle of sustenance—not too little and not too much but a continuing stream of food made available on a steady basis, all the more remarkable because it came during a time of famine when there was much need and want in the land, not ending until the time of the Lord had come.

I chose this verse because it ably represents what has happened in pentecostal historiography during the time that Harrell has participated in its evolution. The early pioneers of pentecostalism would also have liked the verse because it would seem to fit so well with their own interpretation of what they termed "the Latter Rain," loosely a time of spiritual renewal that pentecostals believed would come near the end of time to nurture the church. Using agricultural analogies, pentecostal writers like the prolific educator George Floyd Taylor theorized that early church growth had come from a watering of the Holy Spirit similar to the "early rain" that watered crops shortly after planting. Now, as the crop of God's kingdom neared its maturity for the final harvest, another watering, a "latter rain" was falling. Indeed, many pentecostals argued that they *were* themselves the "Latter Rain" here to bring about revival.[1]

Numerical success for pentecostal denominations, over 10 million adherents in the United States by the year 2000, was generated at least in part by this missionary mentality. The movement's numbers doubled, perhaps even tripled, if the ranks of charismatic Christians, often members of mainline denominations and Roman Catholics influenced by pentecostal theology, were included. Most impressive of all was the international impact. By some estimates, as many as 500 million souls worldwide worshiped under the vast net of churches inspired by the pentecostal revival of a century ago.[2] And, of course, this numerical success ultimately generated historical interest and the assurance that pentecostal historiography would continue. The most authoritative recent summary of the literature begins, "After years of benign neglect, scholarly resources for the study of American Pentecostalism are beginning to tumble off the presses at an astonishing rate. The literature on the subject has become so extensive that bibliographic guides are virtually indispensable."[3]

For the most part, there have been three specific types of historians interested in all things pentecostal and charismatic: (1) those from within the movement, (2) those not exactly in but with roots and a family tradition in the movement, and (3) those outside the movement. We might parse that a bit more, but it will suffice for this treatment.

Those outside the movement were few and far between in the early years. Charles Shumway was an ardent and relatively objective observer in both MA and PhD studies during the second decade of the twentieth century, but most academics simply ignored the movement or tended toward sweeping generalizations.[4] In doing so, they left the early history to the pentecostals themselves. And early pentecostals wrote a lot, though they often mixed history and theology, failing to see very much difference between the sermon and the symposium. From authors like Bennett F. Lawrence, Stanley Frodsham, Donald Gee, Joseph Campbell, Ethel Goss, and John Nichol, the history was written, the names duly recorded.[5]

By the mid-1970s, a talented core of young historians from pentecostal traditions, among them Vinson Synan, William Menzies, Edith Waldvogel (later Blumhofer), and Grant Wacker, had embarked on an intensive study of the merits of the pentecostal past.[6] Some of these remained pentecostal, some did not, but all shared a quiet obsession with their own past—not quite at ease with the history they had been dealt. They struggled with a tradition of record-keepers unwilling to move beyond the pall of names and organizational dates and *historio*-preachers determined somehow to use the past to convert the unbelieving. These young historians, however, were trained to play the game of history by a different set of rules—to leave the preaching to the theologically inclined and to move beyond the chronicling of their forefathers and foremothers. Unlike their predecessors, they understood and consciously tried to follow those rules. This generation would nurture the Society for Pentecostal Studies and its infant journal *Pneuma,* formed in 1971. And, in the end, it was they who benefited most from the resurgence of interest by the outsiders, who, by the 1970s, were beginning to notice the numbers and ask new questions about these brothers and sisters from across the tracks. So when Oxford University Press published Robert Anderson's important *Vision of the Disinherited* in 1979, this generation of historians both embraced and raised objections to elements of his analysis.

Although I was a decade or so younger than these historians, I became one of them—influenced by them and benefiting from their struggles. Like them, I knew names like Oral Roberts, Aimee Semple McPherson, A. A. Allen, and Kathryn Kuhlman. Like them, I had been emboldened yet also embarrassed by the success of these men and women. Like them, my earliest foray into the history of pentecostalism was in part a search for my own understanding of the religious culture I had inherited. And, in the early 1980s, when these older brothers and sisters came to advise me about where I should study and with whom I should work, one name emerged front and center. Why had David Edwin Harrell Jr. made such an impression on them?

Even before Anderson, Harrell—another scholar from outside the ranks—had taken notice of the importance of the pentecostal and charismatic movements. His written contribution has come primarily through two books: *All Things Are Possible: The Healing and Charismatic Revivals in Modern America* (Indiana University Press, 1975) and *Oral Roberts: An American Life* (Indiana University Press, 1985). The first was published while I was in college, taking my first course in pentecostal history under Vinson Synan; the second was researched and written largely while I was a student in the doctoral program at the University of Arkansas, becoming—ironically perhaps—Harrell's first doctoral student. I say ironically because his labor in *All Things Are Possible* led directly to the possibility of our relationship. Those who understood me told me that Harrell was not only the kind of scholar I needed to work with but also was the kind of man who would treat me seriously, the kind of man I could trust with my academic future. So what was it about that book that caused such a dramatic shift in my own life? What was it that had influenced so many like me to respect a man we had not yet met, had not yet shared a meal with, had not yet come to know? How is it that we could trust this historian when so many others left us uneasy?

There are at least three major contributions that Harrell had made in *All Things Are Possible*: (1) He dealt with pentecostals fairly, accepting that they were genuine in their convictions and, importantly for their sense of acceptance, he had portrayed them as a viable part of the American evangelical community. (2) He demonstrated that pentecostalism was significant, that the movement had amounted to something important. Coming from a non-pentecostal authority, this was crucial for pentecostal self-confidence. (3) He validated that pentecostals and the theology they espoused could be studied objectively, with a healthy degree of skepticism moderated by a degree of admiration for their tenacity and considerable list of accomplishments.

Others within the pentecostal scholarly community, and particularly when he was working on the Oral Roberts biography, often asked me: "Is Harrell a Pentecostal?," and, sometimes, "Is Harrell a Christian?" Knowing him to be a decidedly non-pentecostal man of faith still affiliated with the Church of Christ tradition, I could of course answer those questions, but I preferred to leave them unanswered. After all, what greater compliment can a historian have than simply to leave them guessing?

Pentecostals saw in Harrell a genuine scholar, someone from a major university, whose books were published by top academic presses, who saw things their way—at least in the sense that he saw who they were and recognized that their heritage was important, that their existence mattered.

The attraction was apparent from the opening lines of *All Things Are Possible.* Consider the initial thoughts from the preface:

> It has not been easy to be objective about the healing and charismatic religious movements. Healing revivalism invites caricature, but this book is based on the belief that the movement is too important to be handled carelessly or flippantly. My quest for objectivity has led me into the frequent, and perhaps tedious, use of quotations. But there is some advantage in letting the men who know the revival best tell the story. . . . As it happens, I do not share the religious presuppositions of the charismatic revivalists, but in my many conversations with them, I have insisted that my own religious views are, if I do my job properly, irrelevant to the telling of the story.[7]

Intuitively judging that such had not always been the case, pentecostals understood that in Harrell they had someone they could trust to be fair.

All Things Are Possible was the first academic investigation of the pentecostal-inspired healing crusades of the mid-twentieth century. The focus of the book was twofold: First, Harrell explained the dynamic that was the healing revivals from 1947 to 1958. Then he turned his attention to the emergence of an even more profound phenomenon still very much in its infancy during the years the book was written. By 1958 the healing revivals had declined and the more astute of the evangelists (represented especially by Oral Roberts) focused their attention toward general evangelism. This shift occurred alongside the emergence of the charismatic movement, which then became the central point of the revival's efforts, the focus on healing now expanded to include all the gifts of the Spirit. The shift also positioned the evangelists further away from their ties to traditional pentecostal denominations.

Reviews say more thirty years later than they did when they initially appeared—at least they seem more insightful or ridiculous thirty years later. Almost all reviewers of *All Things Are Possible* gave its author high marks for tackling an important and previously ignored topic. Mary Schneider, in *Reviews in American History,* referenced the "meager academically sound number of works dealing with what has been perhaps the most neglected area of American religious history since the relatively recent white discovery of the existence of black churches and black theology."[8] William Martin, in the *Journal of Southern History,* echoed this sentiment by observing that Sydney Ahlstrom's exhaustive *A Religious History of the American People,* published three years earlier, practically ignored the healing evangelists: "[he] mentions none save Oral Roberts and devotes but a single sentence to him, despite the fact that few individuals have ever had an impact on American religion as impressive and, probably, as abiding as has Roberts."[9] Of the omission, the Schneider review concluded that "with Harrell's book this no longer becomes possible. The one fact which perhaps stands out and compels our attention is the vast influence of the healers through the various communications media. When paid subscriptions to revivalists' magazines range in the hundreds of thousands and each reaches the public through radio and/or TV, it is no longer possible to dismiss these revivalists as a fringe phenomenon in American religious culture."[10] In this case, the reviewers clearly recognized what Harrell knew instinctively and what pentecostals had been aching over for decades but probably did not fully comprehend themselves: nothing is more insulting than to be ignored. To paraphrase a B. J. Thomas song: A little bit of press is better than no press, even bad press is better than no press, any kind of press is better than no press at all.

On the matter of fairness, perhaps Martin said it best when he opened his appraisal: "As if to illustrate that, indeed, all things *are* possible, David Edwin Harrell Jr. has produced a book about healing revivalists that takes them seriously and treats them fairly."[11] It was left for Paul Carter, in a review that appeared in the *Journal of American History* in December 1976, to wax most eloquently: "The subject is especially easy for an academic historian to do badly; intellectual aversion to fundamentalist Biblical literalism and to supernaturalism is often combined with an eastern urbanite's distaste for southern—or, more accurately in this case, for sun belt—folkways. Happily, in the present case the book and its author are a perfect match. David Edwin Harrell Jr. has been fair almost to a fault."[12]

But, alas, no one escapes unscathed. A very young Grant Wacker, writing for *Church History* from the Cambridge, Massachusetts, address where he was still in graduate school, acknowledged Harrell to be "consistently judicious and objective" and began by giving the book its due: "As a history of the faith-healing revival, *per se,* the book undoubtedly will stand as the definitive treatment for years to come." But then he took the opportunity to add: "Harrell goes astray, however, in the larger interpretative dimensions of the study. He argues, first, that the independent healing ministries 'were in a large part responsible for the unexpected growth of Pentecostalism in modern America' (p. 4). No student of the history of

Pentecostalism would deny that faith-healing has been an important part of the story, but many will question Harrell's view that healing has been, in effect, the functional backbone of modern Pentecostalism."[13] Even the impressed Martin included amid his praise a note that may have been to a younger Harrell at least a small sting: "Professor Harrell has managed to compress a great deal into a book of only moderate length. His style, though not especially sparkling, is clear, uncluttered, and readable."[14]

Ernest Sandeen, however, in the October 1976 *American Historical Review,* sounded the most disturbing note of criticism. After a cursory summary of the book's content, Sandeen acknowledged Harrell's contribution in registering "a movement that has not previously received scholarly treatment," and noted that "as a biographical dictionary or a reference work, it will serve historians well." But he then surmised that "Harrell has failed to set the movement into a context in which these revivalists can be understood by the student of either social or religious history" and accused the writer of being "so timid in judging the careers of the revivalists that the reader cannot ascertain what the author means to say.... One certainly does not want a simplistic score card of the good and bad guys, but if a historian fails to establish a point of view, he produces, as I fear Harrell has, only a catalog."[15]

Alone in his criticism, Sandeen simply "didn't get it." We pentecostals were frankly tired of having academicians tell us and others who we were, tired of being judged as so much an aberration of American Christianity, tired of having others portray us as childlike innocents or as malicious charlatans. In Harrell we found someone whose words allowed us to speak for ourselves and gave us the benefit of the doubt provided the evidence did not contradict our own words. Although some no doubt would have liked to "convert" Harrell to our ranks, most understood that it was unnecessary, maybe even unwise. In the final analysis, he made us more trusting, less paranoid, and better able to look at ourselves through an objective eye. And that is never bad—always beneficial.

Oral Roberts: An American Life enjoyed a foundation from the source collecting and analysis of *All Things Are Possible,* from whose pages Roberts had emerged as the most fascinating and most adaptable evangelist. In the pages of this splendid biography, Harrell uncovered a complicated personality—one whose talents and demons led to both successes and shortcomings. The biography was most remarkable, I think, because it demonstrated precisely how fair this historian could be. Few in or outside the movement could have interacted with Oral Roberts and come away with the kind of balance that the book revealed. It objectively chronicled the controversy that had swirled around the more flamboyant periods of Roberts's career, from flaps about whether or not people had really been "healed" to the vision of a nine-hundred-foot Jesus ensuring him of the completion of the City of Faith Medical Center.

Again, the reviewers took note. Edwin Gaustad asserted in the *Journal of American History*, "Harrell shows Roberts in his weaknesses and strengths, his moodiness and temper tantrums, his amazing resilience in the face of criticism and adversity."[16] William Martin returned to the pages of the *Journal of Southern History* to assess that "Harrell disagrees with the theology of Pentecostal healing and supernaturally furnished prosperity, finds Roberts himself 'not entirely likable' (p. x), and harbors justifiable doubts about the future of the ministry without Oral at the helm. Yet he is evenhanded in his presentation of the theology, generous in his assessment of Roberts as a sincere and honorable man who genuinely believes God has directed his life, and realistically optimistic that history will prove his ministry to have been of considerably more significance than many may have assumed."[17]

Two years after Harrell's book appeared, Roberts encountered perhaps his sharpest ridicule from both the secular and religious press when he revealed a message from God that he must raise a total of 8 million dollars or else his life on earth would be finished. Although the money reportedly was raised, Roberts announced the closing of the City of Faith less than three years later. Today the official Oral Roberts University website recalls that the City of Faith, "the largest health facility of its kind in the world . . . revolutionized the medical world's concept of primary patient care and the importance of treating the whole person—spirit, mind, and body."[18] The website sees only the positive legacy, and some of Roberts's critics decry the entire episode as a scam, yet in the final analysis, historians get their say. And, in this, Harrell is still right. Roberts will be remembered for a career that catapulted him into the unenviable position as America's second best-known preacher and, given the growth and importance of the pentecostal and charismatic movements worldwide as the twenty-first century dawned, arguably the most influential religious figure of his time.

Harrell's work has spanned many topics in his long and important career. He has written on more than pentecostalism, but his contribution to those of us in pentecostal studies has been vital. And there are other works that we might discuss if there were time: a biography of Pat Robertson and a number of articles with a pentecostal context. In addition, Harrell has been a presence, speaking at conferences and lecturing literally around the globe. *All Things Are Possible* will soon be reissued in an updated edition, a testimony to the book's enduring impact. A forthcoming article on the ministry of India's D. G. Dhinakaran demonstrates his continuing contribution to new scholarship in the pentecostal field. The books, articles, and lectures on pentecostal themes did not make the seemingly bottomless "cruse of oil" that has become pentecostal historiography here in the early years of the present century. But to stop there is to miss the point. Many have written and are writing because of the example set. And not only are they writing, but they are writing with a fairer, more objective pen.

3

David Edwin Harrell Jr. and the History of the Stone-Campbell Tradition

Richard T. Hughes

David Edwin Harrell Jr. has taught me much about the craft of historical writing, about the role of social factors in religious history, and about the multitude of forces that have shaped my own religious tradition, the Churches of Christ. He has published three major books on the Churches of Christ, each of them pioneering in its own right, along with numerous articles that explore various aspects of this tradition. If we wish to define the category of "restoration" more broadly, as indeed we should, then we would include as well his work on American pentecostalism and certain strands of southern evangelicalism. But since James Goff and Charles Wilson explore Harrell's work on those traditions, I will confine my remarks to his work on the history of the Churches of Christ. I must say, however, that Harrell's work on the Churches of Christ has informed and shaped everything he has done over the course of a long career, including his study of pentecostalism, evangelicalism, and southern sectarian movements.

I first encountered Harrell's work in the spring semester of 1967, when I was only twenty-four years old and working on a master's degree in church history at Abilene Christian University. Along with perhaps ten other graduate students, I had enrolled that term in a course the catalog described as "The History of the Restoration Movement." There have been many "restoration movements" in Christian history, but we all understood that this course was special: it was about the history of the Churches of Christ, the tradition to which each of us belonged.

Along the way, the professor required us to read Harrell's first book-length history of that tradition, a volume published in 1966 that bore the title *Quest for a Christian America.*[1] This text was unlike any history of that tradition any of us had ever read. In the first place, it seemed so ruthlessly objective. At that point in time, most histories of this tradition made room for at least some hagiography, but whoever wrote this book seemed more than willing to tell the truth about our church, even when that truth was unflattering.

In the second place, this book argued that social factors helped determine the religious convictions that characterized our tradition. That claim was particularly difficult to swallow, for each of us understood that our church—the Church of Christ—had restored in crucial ways the essential elements of biblical Christianity. For that reason, many in our tradition claimed that the Church of Christ was the one true church outside of which there could be no salvation.

But this fellow Harrell—whoever he was, and none of us had heard his name before—this fellow Harrell seemed to undermine those assumptions by suggesting that economic factors, north/south sectionalism, slavery, and the Civil War helped produce our church and the convictions it held most dear. In a crucial article that Harrell published in 1964, he flatly asserted that the "twentieth-century Churches of Christ are the spirited offspring of the religious rednecks of the post-bellum South."[2]

On the day set aside for discussion of Harrell's book, the professor asked us to speculate regarding the author's theological orientation. To a person, all the students were convinced that Harrell was not a member of the Churches of Christ but probably belonged to the more liberal wing of our movement, the Disciples of Christ. Imagine our shock when the professor informed us that Harrell belonged to the most conservative wing of our tradition.

In 1966, the very year that Harrell published *Quest for a Christian America*—a book that struck the other students and me as a profoundly relativizing text—he also made a presentation at the Disciples of Christ Historical Society in which he spoke frankly about his own religious commitments. There was nothing relativizing about that address. Instead, in that speech, Harrell made the following confession:

> I am a Biblical literalist. I mean by that simply that I believe in a literal and narrow interpretation of the Bible as the Word of God. My aim is the exact restoration of the ancient order of things. It is an article of my faith that the Bible should be, can be, and is literally understandable and that it should lead all men to the same conclusions. . . . Any man who believes that he can find literal truth

> in the Scriptures must also believe that those who do not find the same truth are wrong. What follows is that such people are sinful. The next logical conclusion is that they will go to hell. . . . All members of the Churches of Christ do not have such an attitude, but I do. . . . From my theological point of view, the group to which I belong is the church universal.

In fairness, Harrell continued that address with these words: "This does not imply that I would restrict anyone's right to believe as he pleases. . . . The essence of the philosophy of toleration is a willingness to defend a man's right to free expression even when one has deep convictions to the contrary."[3] Still and all, if my graduate student comrades and I had known of this speech when we read Harrell's book, *Quest for a Christian America,* we might well have been stunned into senselessness.

The truth is, David Edwin Harrell Jr. has been an enigma for countless scholars over many, many years. In 1975 I organized a conference at Pepperdine University around the theme "Restitution, Dissent, and Renewal."[4] Two of the speakers were David Edwin Harrell and Sidney E. Mead. In the course of his presentation, Harrell confessed that for religious reasons he had voted only once in his life, an action he now had come to regret.[5] That confession touched off a minor conference furor. Many in the audience were appalled. One young woman called his position a "cop out." Sidney Mead was especially aghast, and in a letter to me dated June 9, 1975, expressed nothing short of outrage. "How one can be chairman of a History dept. in a State University, taking all the benefits of that position, and yet renounce all responsibility for the conduct of the institution(s) that make it possible is beyond my present understanding. No wonder the girl called it a 'cop out.' . . . I feel uneasy in the presence of persons with that moral standard."

But Sidney Mead had virtually no understanding of what made Harrell tick. Indeed, few have. Most who have known his historical work—and have also known the extraordinarily conservative nature of his religious commitments—have puzzled over how a man can be such a scrupulous social historian but refuse to accept the relativizing implications of the history that he writes. Some have unkindly described Harrell as intellectually schizophrenic.

But herein lies the irony; it is simply not true that Harrell's scholarship and religious commitments are out of sync with each other. To the contrary, his religious commitments have so thoroughly informed his scholarship that one cannot understand the historiographic principles that have shaped his work unless one understands something of his religious commitments.

Thus a word about the religious tradition that has shaped his life and work is in order. In the nineteenth century, Churches of Christ committed themselves to the restoration of what they described as original New Testament Christianity. Central to their understanding of the ancient faith was a profoundly democratic and congregational polity. In that context, Churches of Christ resisted even the slightest hint of centralization. And for all those years, Churches of Christ—for the most part—were economically deprived and marginal to the larger culture. In a word, they were cultural outsiders.

But following World War I, the mainstream of Churches of Christ began its quest for denominational respectability, a quest that accelerated following World War II. In the 1940s and early 1950s, that quest led hundreds of congregations to construct substantial—and sometimes lavish—buildings on important streets in reputable neighborhoods. It led Church of Christ–related colleges to push for their own brand of respectability as they sought accreditation from secular accrediting agencies. It even led some Churches of Christ to court the support and protection of the federal government in the context of a minor crisis involving Church of Christ missionaries overseas. "By the end of the 1940s," Harrell notes, "most leaders in the churches no longer felt a deep sense of alienation from their culture; indeed, they had become breast-beating American patriots."[6]

But there is more. As Churches of Christ intensified their quest for denominational respectability, they began to develop cooperative structures and parachurch organizations that flew in the face of the radically democratic polity they had cultivated throughout the nineteenth century. In the face of this transition, a conservative group of individuals and congregations began to protest these changes. These people shared much with the mainstream Churches of Christ, especially in their commitment to legalism, literalism, and a profoundly rational reading of the biblical text. But they categorically rejected the mainstream drive for denominational respectability and held tenaciously to the conviction that the church of the restoration—the true church of the Bible—could never attain respectability but would always work at the margins of the dominant culture. In a word, these people both claimed and prized the role of cultural outsider.

The mainstream of Churches of Christ unkindly referred to these radicals as "antis," shorthand for "anti-institutional" Churches of Christ, and finally drummed these churches out of the fold of the mainstream tradition only twelve years before Harrell wrote his first book, *Quest for a Christian America.* From the inception of that tradition, Harrell has not only belonged to the "anti-institutional" Churches of Christ, he has also been a leader among those congregations.

In a review of Harrell's work published in 2004, Samuel S. Hill observed that Harrell "does not work with a self-conscious reference to what exactly historiography is about."[7] In that judgment, Hill, I think, was wrong. It seems to me that Harrell has worked with a profoundly self-conscious historiographic awareness, and his commitment to the principles of the anti-institutional Churches of Christ has both informed and supported that awareness at every step along the way. Recognizing Harrell's penchant for objectivity, Hill sensed the truth of this judgment when he wrote that Harrell's concern for obedience to divine commands "transfers rather readily . . . to religious legalism and total dedication to objectivity in the practice of the historian's craft."[8]

But Harrell's religious commitments have shaped his historiography in ways that far transcend his penchant for historical objectivity. The book that finally makes this clear is Harrell's *The Churches of Christ in the Twentieth Century: Homer Hailey's Personal Journey of Faith.* While Harrell treats in this book the twentieth-century history of the mainstream Churches of Christ, he also relates the history of the anti-institutional movement in substantial detail. He illustrates the history of that movement by telling the story of Homer Hailey, an anti-institutional leader and a man, as Harrell notes, with "a strong sense of cultural separation."[9] Harrell notes that the anti-institutional churches as a whole were committed to an "amorphous sense of alienation and world rejection" and to the preservation of "cultural dissonance." Most important of all, Harrell notes in his preface to this book that "this narrative is *my story.*"[10] One doesn't have to read between the lines too terribly far to begin to see that Harrell regards himself as a cultural outsider.

Surely, this outsider consciousness is responsible for the specific religious movements that Harrell has chosen to chronicle over the course of a long career—Churches of Christ, pentecostals, and other sectarian movements in the American South. But the outsider consciousness of the anti-institutional Churches of Christ has also contributed to the fact that Harrell has quite deliberately embraced the methods of social history rather than the methods of intellectual history. Harrell has always believed that social dynamics, not quarrels over doctrine and theology, stood at the heart of the rupture between the mainstream Churches of Christ and their anti-institutional counterparts.

Harrell embraced the principles of social history prior to his introduction to the anti-institutional Churches of Christ. But his experience in that tradition has only buttressed his sociological orientation as a historian. Harrell writes that "at some level, almost all noninstitutional leaders sensed that a social chasm had developed in the movement, and a few saw this new economic and cultural diversity as more ominous than the raging doctrinal debate."[11] Precisely for this reason, Harrell notes, these churches "were more likely to appeal to cultural commentary than to textual argument in their criticisms of the 'on the march' mentality" of the mainstream Churches of Christ.[12] And Harrell too—as a child of this tradition—has been far "more likely to appeal to cultural commentary than to textual argument" in his studies of Churches of Christ and of other sectarian movements in the American South.

In an address delivered at Abilene Christian University in 1988, Harrell observed, "I have long been convinced that ideas are not the primary movers of history, but that history reaches out for the ideas needed at the time."[13] He found support for this conviction in the anti-institutional Churches of Christ and has always claimed, therefore, that doctrinal and theological disputes are only symptoms of much deeper social convulsions.

One more question begs for an answer, and it is this: How can Harrell be such a scrupulous social historian but apparently refuse to see the theological implications of the history he writes? One would think, for example, that Harrell's insights into the power of the various social forces that have shaped the Churches of Christ might lead him to question his conviction that his particular tradition is the one true and universal church. How is it that he apparently keeps sociological analysis so separate from intellectual understanding and theological conviction?

The answer to that question lies, once again, in the history of the anti-institutional movement and even in the larger history of the Churches of Christ. Actually, the Churches of Christ have always had a strong intellectual component, grounded in their roots in the Anglo-American Enlightenment. At the same time, anti-intellectual sentiments have flourished in this tradition, thanks to the movement's bias toward populism, literalism, and legalism, and its refusal to take seriously the reality of its own history.[14]

Harrell calls attention to this reality when he writes that "a populist confidence in the ability of the common person to understand truth, often accompanied by overt anti-intellectual prejudices, made members of the churches of Christ wary of education and pretentious scholarship."[15] That populist, anti-intellectual prejudice also made members of Churches of Christ deeply suspicious of theology. Indeed, they typically claimed to have no theology but the Bible. In this, Homer Hailey was typical. "Hailey's religious faith," Harrell writes, "was always practical and nonspeculative. He thought deeply about the mysteries of Christianity, but he was uncomfortable in opaque theological waters."[16]

As a true child of the anti-institutional wing of Churches of Christ, so is David Edwin Harrell Jr. uncomfortable in opaque theological waters. For years Harrell has brooded over the bias against theology that has characterized the anti-institutional Churches of Christ and what that bias might mean for his work as a social historian. He is not naive.

Harrell wrote in 1988, "If disinterest in theology and speculative thought is anti-intellectualism, then the label fits."[17] Harrell understands and accepts the fact, in his own work at least, that theology and social history must stand apart from each other. He made this very point in his address to the Disciples of Christ Historical Society in 1966 when he pointed to Francis Bacon's understanding of "double truth." According to Harrell, Bacon "held that philosophy should be kept separate from theology. The purpose of philosophy was practical: to give men mastery over the forces of nature by means of scientific discoveries and inventions. Theology consisted of that which is known by revelation." Then Harrell wrote, "There are certain advantages in such a schizoid view of truth. In a world of scientific relativism, of political uncertainty, of social injustice, and individual brutality, it is no small comfort to be able to turn to a citadel of truth." For this reason, he argued, "there is no essential relation between the mind of man and the faith of man in this life."[18]

Harrell's reference to "a citadel of truth" raises an issue that has surfaced time and again in the course of this analysis—Harrell's utter commitment to historical objectivity and his firm belief that historical objectivity is possible. In taking that position he obviously parts company with perhaps the majority of historians who would argue that historical objectivity is a noble ideal but finally an illusion.

How should we understand Harrell's commitment to historical objectivity when so many historians reject that possibility out of hand? There are two considerations at work here. First, Harrell's commitment to historical objectivity is part and parcel—as Samuel S. Hill has pointed out—of his claim that his small, countercultural church embraces a pure, unvarnished "citadel of truth." In other words, he assumes the possibility of "historical objectivity" for the same reason he assumes that his own sectarian movement can embody the whole of Christian truth.

But why—and this is our second consideration—does Harrell seem to have no capacity to challenge or question that assumption? The answer to this question is rooted in his rejection of theology. After all, Christian theology begins and ends with the claim that since God alone is God, the most important assertion that might be made about human beings is that we might be wrong. But by rejecting theology out of hand, Harrell has effectively insulated himself from any serious challenge to his conviction that historical objectivity is genuinely possible.

As we near the end of this analysis, then, how might we summarize what we have said about David Edwin Harrell, the historian?

The truth is that his commitment to the antitheological and anti-institutional Churches of Christ has shaped this man's career in profound and far-reaching ways. That allegiance has helped determine who and what he would study, the methods he would bring to bear in his analysis of those traditions, and ironically, even the way he separates history from theology and personal faith.

Harrell knows precisely who he is. He movingly explained his powerful sense of self to a rapt audience gathered at Abilene Christian University in 1988. That very sense of self has determined not only who he is as a man but also who he is as a historian. And that sense of self has everything to do with the restoration vision. "I am a restorer," he said,

> unbowed, undaunted, extremist, and eccentric—a period piece in a Disciples of Christ movement grown increasingly uncomfortable with the intellectual, social, and psychological pitfalls of restoring New Testament Christianity. The centerpiece of my intellectual universe is biblical primitivism, a search for the first pure truths and ordinances. I am seeking that illusive, pristine image of Christianity as it came from the mind of God. You say it is not there; it is an illusion. I have decided to seek it anyway. We live in a world of illusions. You say I will not find it because I carry on my back the baggage of my own past, of the culture in which I live, of the language with which I think. Self-consciously and with as much self-awareness as possible, I have decided to try. You say I shall fail and be disillusioned. So far, I have not. . . . It has been a rigorous journey, but I know existentially no other way. The search has served me

> well, and should you come to look for me, you will find me a bit further down the same road.[19]

In the case of Harrell the historian, the road of biblical primitivism has been a productive road to travel. It has led him to embrace the highest standards of historical scholarship. It has engendered in his mind and heart a passion to tell the stories of the religiously and economically dispossessed. It has confirmed his commitment to the methods of social history. And because he has traveled that road so long and so well, he has enriched the rest of us in ways he cannot possibly know or comprehend. Thank you, Ed, for the gift of your splendid work.

4

David Edwin Harrell Jr. and the Broadening of Southern Religious Studies

Charles Reagan Wilson

David Edwin Harrell Jr. is one of the founding fathers in the study of religion in the American South, and his legacy was to broaden the field into productive areas that have become central aspects of the study of not only southern religion but also the history of the South itself. The academic study of religion in the South took a giant leap in the 1960s, with what John B. Boles has called "the discovery of southern religious history."[1] The predominant focus for that field became the hegemony of evangelical Protestantism, and several generations of scholars have made it a lively area of study. We now have an encyclopedia of religion in the South in its second edition, an online scholarly journal, a series of award-winning monographs, many edited proceedings from academic conferences, collections of scholarly articles, and a young generation of interdisciplinary scholars who are raising new issues beyond those that have dominated the field.[2]

From early on, Harrell raised questions about the single-minded focus on mainstream evangelical Protestantism in the South, and his work has led to better appreciation by scholars of the role of the American restoration movement in the region and the importance of social class within southern Protestantism. He has not only broadened our understanding of southern religion but also has helped broaden our understanding of the southern identity itself, especially the relationship to it of social groups who often did not have the power of elites to shape the region's predominant mythology and ideology and yet were very clearly southerners. He has characterized his own work as the exploration of the underside of southern religion; I would add that he has explored the borders and boundaries of religion within the South and between the South and other parts of the nation.

Harrell was indeed part of the discovery of southern religion, one of many southerners of his generation who engaged their own religious heritages, drew from their institutional settings of graduate study, and made use of available archival material. "I think that my career as a historian was shaped largely by the insights I learned before I was twenty years old," Harrell has written.[3] His childhood and youth in Florida and south Georgia, his life and work on the farm, his growing up in a religious family with many sectarian branches—all gave him an experiential advantage in asking research questions and taking his subjects seriously. Harrell did his graduate work at Vanderbilt University, the most important institutional context for the early development of the field of southern religious study. Walter B. Posey was a mentor to many graduate students there, encouraging them to follow in his own work on religion in the South, which had led to his publications on Baptists, Methodists, and Presbyterians in the region. Several Vanderbilt students had written dissertations on religion in the South before Harrell, including Rufus Spain and Kenneth K. Bailey. Harrell's research methodology was rooted in social history, a field that came of age in the 1960s. Another Vanderbilt scholar, Henry Lee Swint, taught social history, and Harrell gives credit to him for his own approach.[4]

These developments in the 1960s were a departure from much earlier work on religion in the region, which had often not been produced by academic historians but by denominational scholars who were sometimes most interested in the institutional history of their church but not broader issues of religion and the region's overall history. Bailey's book, *Southern White Protestantism in the Twentieth Century,* which appeared in 1964, is usually seen as the beginning of modern southern religious studies. Bailey had done systematic research in primary sources of the Baptists, Methodists, and Presbyterians, and he sketched the interdenominational profile of a shared Protestant culture that had not only long dominated the South but still did in the 1960s. Samuel Hill's *Southern Churches in Crisis* (1966) further advanced the context for Harrell's forthcoming initial scholarship. Hill's methodological skills in combining history, sociology, and theology offered a sophisticated analysis of white Protestantism. In a way he banished the ghost of H. L. Mencken, who had once complained that the South was "a cesspool of Baptists" and "a miasma of Methodists." W. J. Cash, who often operated in Mencken's orbit, wrote insightfully of the South's tribal god, but he did not take time to decipher the complexity of religion in the South, nor did C. Vann Woodward, whose landmark *Origins of the New South* (1951) gave sophisticated attention to the postbellum South's economics, politics, and society but devoted only a handful of pages to religion. Hill's study deconstructed the historical origins of a distinctive southern religious tradition that was overwhelmingly evangelical. He labeled the overriding concern for sin and salvation as the central theme in the region's spiritual life, a characterization that still predominates. Hill also stressed that the individualistic, conversion-centered ethos of popular evangelicalism led its adherents into defense of the southern status quo, a point of view that led John Eighmy to use the phrase "churches in cultural captivity," a theme that has had a long hegemony in southern religious studies.[5] Race has loomed large as a compelling issue of analysis, seen from the passionate tone of Samuel Hill's 1966 book, which was not only a scholarly study but also had the quality of a jeremiad, pointing out the moral issues involved in the South's struggle for desegregation. The criticism by scholars in southern religious studies of the failure of the South's white churches to deal fairly with black southerners reflected the overall viewpoint of other historians studying the centrality of racial issues to the history of the South in general.[6]

One of Harrell's earliest works explored the issue of race, opening new avenues in examining the relationship between black and white religious southerners. *White Sects and Black Men in the Recent South* (1971) looked not at the mainstream, powerful southern evangelical churches but at such groups as the Free Will Baptists, the Primitive Baptists, Cumberland Presbyterians, Churches of Christ, and various pentecostal and holiness churches. He stressed the sometimes-unorthodox attitudes of working-class and lower-class churches in the Jim Crow South, which did not always abide by the segregationist strictures of the region. He stressed that their racial views were "primarily related to class values rather than theological presuppositions."[7] One of the book's reviewers noted that Harrell illustrated examples of how "poor whites and blacks have lived in close association with relative harmony and even neighborliness and these associations bred a more easy-going attitude toward the integration of their churches than that found among more upward mobile white Southerners."[8] John Boles wrote that the book established Harrell as a pioneer, in particular, of the academic study of the pentecostal-holiness movement in the South.[9]

Harrell would soon pursue his studies of the social class dimensions of religion in the South, but the other focus of his early scholarship was the American restoration movement. His two-volume work on the Disciples of Christ/Christian Church was a model of new denominational history, placing the story of the church in the context of American history, tracing institutional developments, exploring the philosophical assumptions of the founders and later leaders, and using social history to give voice to lay people as well as church leaders. He showed a sharp understanding of the ideal of the primitive church, the disputational nature of the tradition, and the sociological underpinnings of the churches in rural areas and cities in the nineteenth century. He placed the church in the context of southern history, but a southern history that was a part of the nation's religious history. His careful exploration of the regional divisions of the Christian Church in the mid-nineteenth century illuminated the adaptation of local congregations to North and South during the Civil War, without a formal institutional division. One of the earlier academic historians of southern religion and Harrell's mentor, Walter Posey, reviewed the two books on the Disciples of Christ in the *Journal of Southern History*, praising them both. He noted of the second volume: "The author with great skill has analyzed and appraised the complex sociological forces that finally divided the Disciples into conservative southern and liberal northern groups."[10]

Harrell's interest in the restoration movement would continue, and he remained active in one of its leading groups, the Churches of Christ. His research interests moved, though, into new areas, reflecting his early insights about the lived experiences of the southerners with whom he had grown up. "As I thought back on my own foray into the pulpits of black Churches of Christ, and even more, as I remembered the Pentecostal world of my aunts and uncles in south Georgia, it seemed to me that there was another racial and religious cosmos in the South," one that did not resemble the evangelically dominant, racially obsessed churches that other historians were examining.[11] To understand this tradition, he read the sociological literature about the South, giving him historical insights on the predicament of poor whites and why their religion was so central to understanding them. Indeed, most reviewers of his work in general come back to his sociological approach to explaining religious groups in the South, a particular interdisciplinary contribution to southern religious studies that has placed Harrell in the company of Liston Pope, among others. From his reading and research he concluded by the early 1970s that "southern religion was much more diverse than generally portrayed, as was southern society." His conclusion stressed social class as a central issue, as he rejected the claims by educated ministers and middle-class denominations that they alone spoke for the South.[12]

In 1975 Harrell published *All Things Are Possible,* a study of the healing revival of the late 1940s and 1950s. The region's hegemonic evangelical groups dismissed the revival, if they noted it at all, but Harrell saw its significance in the dramatic post–World War II growth of pentecostalism. The book was noteworthy for, in Harrell's words, "employing a style and tone that was neither dismissive nor judgmental." Or, as sociologist William Martin wrote, "As if to illustrate that, indeed, all things *are* possible, David Edwin Harrell Jr. had produced a book about healing revivalists that takes them seriously and treats them fairly." Using quotations from his extensive interviews and primary documents produced by the revivalists, he traced the history of the healing revival, examined its principal doctrines, and showed how the revival broadened its early cultural base and expanded into new areas by the mid-1950s. He acknowledged the presence of charlatans among the revivalists but put them into perspective among many other ministers who tried honestly to pursue their beliefs. He pioneered in documenting this landmark revival in the growth of pentecostal influence. Martin paid tribute to Harrell for following "a sawdust trail apparently hitherto unknown to most of his colleagues."[13]

Harrell's work on pentecostalism took him out of the South. The healing revival was a national story, not just a southern one, but it was surely of the South as well. This was a working-class and poor South and geographically a border South with epicenters in places like Oklahoma, Texas, and Missouri. His research on the healing revival had taken him to research collections at Oral Roberts University in Tulsa, and his biographical study of Oral Roberts relentlessly examined the regional and national context for that minister's work. Reviewers noted that Harrell disagreed with many aspects of Roberts's theology but was evenhanded in his treatment of him. Moreover, he allowed those affected by Roberts's healing ministry to tell their stories, coming out of extensive interviews. Harrell wrote another biography of a major pentecostal figure, Pat Robertson, as well. Wayne Flynt noted that the strength of the book is that "Harrell understands Pentecostal religion as well as any academician. Beyond understanding he takes the subject seriously." Harrell can explain Robertson's conversion experience and his baptism of the Holy Spirit with authenticity. Like his other work, this book is cast more in terms of the sociology of religion than Robertson's theological fine-tuning. One comes away from it understanding how dispensational premillennialism underpins Robertson's worldview, but also how people in social groups appropriate religion's meanings.[14]

Even though much of Harrell's work on pentecostalism moves beyond the southern regional context, it is part of his enormous contribution to southern religious studies. He has written that the pentecostal movements and people he has studied "were an extension of the southern religious experience. Pentecostalism had strong southern roots and flourished in the South in the years after World War II." The preachers he studies spoke with pronounced southern accents and were often interpreted as southerners by the national culture. His argument is that after World War II, southern religion, which importantly included southern forms of pentecostalism, "had been exported to the entire nation, indeed to the entire world, by these evangelists through crusades and the use of the media."[15]

Harrell has recently returned to his other major contribution to southern religious studies, the restoration movement. His book on Homer Hailey and the Churches of Christ in the twentieth century is a masterful study of a religious movement that was long overlooked by many scholars but which has now gained impressive analysis by historians. The book is an experimental biography of sorts, half biography and half analytical study of the Churches of Christ. To add to its complexity, it is a deeply personal story, with Harrell as not only author but also participant in some of the church debates that have been central to its development. What is its significance specifically for southern religious studies? Harrell again is working the borders of the South's mainstream. Hailey himself is more westerner than southerner, born in Texas, growing up in southwestern Arizona, and returning to Arizona in retirement. But the Southwest is, by definition, partly southern. My own example may be relevant here. My family on both sides was from middle Tennessee, and my mother had been raised Baptist and my father Church of Christ. We moved to El Paso, Texas, when I was nine years old, a very western city, with a strong Hispanic imprint that, in those days at least, was very different from middle Tennessee. But we easily found Churches of Christ to worship at, and I still remember a Southern Baptist Convention congregation down the street from us, with its church sign including a nice southern hospitality welcome: "A friendly Southern Baptist Church." The Churches of Christ in the Southwest were populated by displaced southerners from places like middle Tennessee, and ties to institutions like David Lipscomb College in Nashville and, closer to home, Abilene Christian College were strong.

Moreover, the Churches of Christ were the upcountry, hill country, border South manifestation of the American restoration movement, as distinct from the Disciples of Christ, with its stronger midwestern roots.[16]

Harrell's book on the Churches of Christ picks up where his two-volume study of the nineteenth-century restoration movement ended, but with the focus now on the group that has arguably become the deepest repository of restoration-primitivist theology and one whose roots are in a working-class and middle-class South, often with its clearest manifestations in areas that were strongholds in the older South of a yeoman culture. Homer Hailey occupied the mainstream of Churches of Christ outlooks and methods through the 1940s, until increasing pressures afterward toward what we might cautiously generalize as modernization brought the Churches of Christ closer toward denominationalism. The result was separation and the recognition of the noninstitutional Churches of Christ. Harrell has written that the book provides "a theological and sociological road map through the schismatic and convoluted history of one of the South's most successful religious groups in the twentieth century." He also sees it as his "most intimately personal piece of historical writing, telling a story in which I am an actor and, at times, a partisan spokesman."[17]

This recent publication, then, comes full circle and gathers together many of the thematic concerns that have been central to Harrell's contributions to southern religious studies. He has illuminated a once little known and appreciated religious group and made it part of the agenda for the continued study of religion in the South. Whether the restoration movement, pentecostalism, or sectarian groups in general that demonstrate the significance of social class concerns to fully understanding religion in the South, Harrell's topics for research have expanded the boundaries of southern religious studies. He has been our guide through a complex world and unveiled it for us. "The divisions in the American restoration movement," he writes, "sparked fractious debates and manufactured a body of arguments that is an almost impenetrable maze to outsiders." Their arguments, he adds, "have been nuanced by history and embodied language and logical differentiations foreign to traditional evangelical theology."[18] Harrell has helped us to see those nuances of history and to decipher the language that has often been outside the mainstream of the evangelical Protestantism that has dominated the South. Never again, though, can we speak of "southern religion" without including restorationism, pentecostalism, and Harrell's other concerns. Reviewers have often commented on the depth of his research, and one of his contributions has been to not only go through previously unused archival material but also to guide future students to primary sources through extensive endnotes, bibliographical reviews, and his own interviews. His work has combined the sociological and the personal in ways that mirror the work of his generation of historians of southern religion and yet that reflect his distinctive experiences as a southerner from a certain social group, religious background, and geographical place within the American South. He recalled that when he was a young faculty member at the University of Georgia, he would often lunch with other southern historians. "Those of us who were southerners," he says, "probed our own southern lives." Harrell has continued to probe his life and the lives of those southerners he studies with objectivity and appreciation.[19]

PART II

5
The Midas Touch
Kenneth E. Hagin and the Prosperity Gospel

Scott Billingsley

Humble Beginnings

By his own account Kenneth Hagin's life was nothing short of a miracle. After barely surviving his premature birth in 1917, he then suffered from a congenital heart defect until he was a teenager. In 1933 he had a near-death experience during which his heart stopped three times and he received "visions" of what hell was like. He remained bedridden for several months, studying his Bible and pondering his mortality. Then, on a hot summer day in 1934, he pulled himself out of bed and declared to all who would listen that he was the recipient of divine healing.[1] Thus began the life and ministry of Kenneth E. Hagin. Although he did not share the celebrity of other charismatic evangelists, such as Oral Roberts and Pat Robertson, Hagin became one of the most influential religious leaders in post–World War II America as a teacher of an entire generation of charismatics.[2] Through his books, crusades, and Rhema Bible Training Center he propounded the prosperity message, which provided the theological and philosophical foundation for most charismatic ministers at the end of the twentieth century. This teaching—generally labeled the "Word of Faith" message—permeated charismatic theology and even found its way into mainstream Protestant thought. Although Hagin was not the first to embrace the principles of the prosperity gospel, he has been widely credited with fully developing and popularizing them. The Word of Faith philosophy became one of the most important—and most criticized—hallmarks of the modern charismatic movement, which was spawned in the 1960s from the healing revivals of the previous decade.

A fresh wave of revivalism swept onto the American religious scene in the years following World War II. In the 1950s healing evangelists such as Oral Roberts, William Branham, and A. A. Allen brought a renewed sense of excitement to the pentecostal movement that it had not seen in nearly half a century. They introduced a new type of celebrity—the televangelist—to American audiences; created huge, independent ministries; and often challenged traditional sexual, social, and racial mores. But the healing revival was fraught with controversy. The mainstream media caricatured many ministers as being little more than religious hucksters, and mainline denominations and other religious groups criticized their showmanship and discounted their miraculous claims. The 1960s witnessed the rise of the charismatic revival, which achieved a greater level of sophistication and respectability among American Christian churches than the pentecostal and healing movements had. Many mainline Protestants and Catholics came to accept the legitimacy of the supernatural "gifts of the spirit," such as glossolalia and divine healing, and a new type of minister emerged whose organizational and teaching skills were often more important than his or her speaking ability.[3] These teachers and organizers led charismatics and pentecostals into the American religious mainstream. From the 1970s onward, "spirit-filled" Christians joined forces politically and culturally with conservative evangelicals, making the charismatic/pentecostal branch one of the fastest growing segments of American evangelicalism.

Kenneth Hagin's friend and contemporary, Oral Roberts, was among the few leaders who made the transition from the healing revival to the charismatic revival, providing the movement with a visible spokesman who garnered the respect and admiration of mainline evangelical leaders. Historian David Edwin Harrell Jr. argued in 1985 that "Oral Roberts has been one of the most influential religious leaders in the world in the twentieth century."[4] The leadership and publicity he provided to the pentecostal and charismatic movements over a fifty-year period were immensurable. He led the healing revival of the 1950s and managed to avoid the devastating scandals that either ruined or severely hampered the careers of other evangelists. He recognized early the changing nature of that movement, and he adjusted his message and methods to stay on the cutting edge of the charismatic revival. More than any other leader, Roberts bridged the gaps that separated pentecostals from charismatics and charismatics from evangelicals. He was one of the few people whom nearly all "spirit-filled" Christians respected and looked to for leadership.

Other ministers, however, were also important to the emergence and growth of the charismatic movement, despite never gaining the celebrity that Roberts enjoyed. Herein lies Kenneth Hagin's legacy. Although not as famous as Roberts, Hagin made contributions to the charismatic movement that were nearly—if not equally—as important as Roberts's. His prosperity message provided the theological foundation that supported the movement in the last quarter of the twentieth century. He offered stability to the revival by creating lasting institutions whereby thousands of charismatic leaders were trained. And he maintained a good reputation and generally avoided the controversies that plagued so many other evangelists. His most significant achievement, however, was the influence he had on the rise of African American—and to a lesser extent female—charismatic ministers in the United States and abroad. Oral Roberts noted in 1977 that "the next great outpouring of the Holy Spirit, and the mighty healing power of God, is to be upon black people," and Kenneth Hagin's prosperity message proved to be the core teaching for many of these preachers.[5]

Hagin began his preaching career in 1934 as the pastor for a small community church near his hometown of McKinney, Texas, and, because he believed in divine healing, associated himself with "full gospel" Christians in the area. Raised a Baptist, he was at first skeptical of the pentecostal practice of speaking in tongues, but he soon became convinced that glossolalia was a legitimate supernatural experience for modern Christians. He was "baptized in the Holy Spirit" in April 1937, and a year later he was ordained as a pentecostal minister in the Assemblies of God denomination. In the ensuing decade he pastored small pentecostal churches in Texas, and in 1949 he became a traveling healing evangelist, experiencing modest success in the 1950s. He did not, however, conduct major tent crusades like some of his more famous contemporaries, including Roberts, Branham, and Allen. Hagin was a soft-spoken, unassuming minister who, according to David Harrell, had "a homey and humorous Texas" preaching style. He avoided publicity and did not seem interested in building a large empire. Even after he achieved greater success in the 1970s and 1980s, he led a modest yet comfortable lifestyle, and, despite criticism of his theology, he maintained a reputation as an honest and sincere man.[6]

As early as 1950 Hagin recognized that his place in the healing and charismatic revivals would be that of teacher. Hoping to reach a broader audience, he relinquished his credentials as a pentecostal minister in 1962, formed his own evangelistic association, and began to focus on his "calling" as a teacher. In the 1960s he became a popular speaker with the Full

Gospel Businessmen's Fellowship International, holding independent meetings throughout the country. He and other new leaders, such as Gordon Lindsay and John Osteen, brought much-needed teaching skills to the charismatic revival, which had not been present in the healing revival of the 1950s. These teachers helped stabilize the neo-pentecostal movement, and they provided a sense of respectability that it previously lacked.[7]

Positive Confession

When the scandals of the healing revival ebbed after the 1950s and the charismatic movement attained respectability among mainstream American Christians in the 1960s, Hagin's teaching about divine healing and prosperity became a focal point for both proponents and critics of the neo-pentecostal revival. The prosperity message found expression in the late twentieth century in what came to be called the Word of Faith movement. This subset of the charismatic movement garnered considerable attention and became a lightning rod for controversy. The basic tenets of the faith message—sometimes called "positive confession"—were that Christians should: (1) study the Bible to determine God's will for their lives, (2) verbally confess God's promise for a particular need, and (3) believe that God had already provided a solution to their problem. Faithful Christians, the argument continued, recognized that they were entitled not only to eternal life in the hereafter, but that divine health and prosperity were also part of the blessing they received through Jesus's death on the cross.[8] Rooted in the nineteenth-century metaphysical teachings of evangelist E. W. Kenyon, Hagin's faith message went a step further by formulating "laws of prosperity to be rehearsed daily by persons seeking health and wealth."[9] He maintained that when a Christian spoke aloud a word from the Bible, that word took "on the creative power of God" and God would give that person whatever she asked.[10] Critics charged that this "name-it-and-claim-it" theology, as it was derisively called, cited biblical passages out of context and distorted traditional pentecostal teachings on divine health and prosperity.

Although positive confession was the cornerstone of Hagin's message, he tried to maintain a moderate position theologically and to avoid "some of the extreme positions taken by some in the faith movement."[11] Kenneth Hagin Jr. defended this position in 1981: "Neither Dad nor I have ever taught that being a Christian means you'll never have any problems. The devil will always try to hinder you but you have authority over the devil through the Word of God. . . . I get so tired of Rhema students who talk about houses and Cadillacs. . . . Thank God, God has provided us prosperity. But the Church doesn't exist for Christian prosperity. The Church of the Lord Jesus Christ exists for those who are locked in the chains of Satan himself."[12]

Kenneth Hagin tried to avoid polemics and generally did not respond to his critics, which were certainly not in short supply.[13] Much of the criticism focused on the potential, and real, excesses of this theology and some of its proponents. Charles Farah, a professor at Oral Roberts University in the early 1980s, characterized the faith message as "a kind of heavenly butler, [that] twists true Biblical faith into an almost magic formula."[14] Michael Horton, editor of *The Agony of Deceit,* framed his critique in the context of late twentieth-century American culture and in contrast to the cultural separatism of earlier generations of pentecostals: "It is appropriate that a prosperity gospel be born in the hedonistic, self-centered, get-rich-quick milieu of modern American society. We are, by nature, pagan. Either our religion will transform us or we will transform our religion to suit our sympathies."[15]

Hagin's good reputation, modest lifestyle, and affable personality allowed him to rise above most controversies surrounding the Word of Faith movement. Despite the attacks on his theology and the criticism that other prosperity preachers faced, Hagin was a moderating force in the charismatic movement. His influence was subtler than other independent evangelists, and he did not receive the same sort of public scrutiny that other leaders, such as Oral Roberts, Joyce Meyer, and Benny Hinn, received. He continued to speak at his annual Campmeeting, publish his *Word of Faith* magazine, and propound his message on his radio and television shows until his death in 2003. But his Rhema Bible Training Center was his most effective tool, producing thousands of graduates who preached prosperity and divine health all over the world. He was also able to promote some of the up-and-coming stars of the charismatic movement.

The Faith Movement

Although the prosperity message had deep roots in the holiness and pentecostal traditions, Kenneth Hagin is commonly regarded as the father of the modern faith movement. In a sympathetic but fair critique of this ideology, charismatic minister and theologian Derek E. Vreeland noted: "The theological systems of the various word of faith ministries, churches and faith teachers lack precise similarity. The faith theology of Hagin differs somewhat from the theology of [Kenneth] Copeland, etc. This presents a methodological problem in identifying what is 'word of faith theology.' The most efficient analysis and reconstruction of word of faith theology proper is to concentrate on the theology of Kenneth Hagin in particular. The various faith ministries may lack systematic cohesion, but a common denominator can be found in the influence of Hagin."[16] Kenneth Copeland, Buddy Harrison, and John Osteen were but a few of the prominent ministers whom Hagin influenced in the 1960s and '70s. In turn, these men spawned their own theological offspring. Copeland mentored one of the most renowned black ministers, Atlanta pastor and evangelist Creflo Dollar. Harrison, who was also Hagin's son-in-law, had a profound impact on the charismatic movement through the Harrison House Publishing Company, which he founded in 1975. Many, if not most, of the major charismatic evangelists in the last quarter of the twentieth century used Harrison House to promote their books and ministries.[17] John Osteen's son, Joel, became a prominent pastor, evangelist, and author at the turn of the twenty-first century. His Lakewood Church in Houston, Texas, has a reported weekly attendance of 28,000, his weekly television broadcast can be seen on numerous networks in the United States and abroad, and his book *Your Best Life Now* (Warner Faith, 2004) quickly became a national best seller.[18]

In 1990, *Charisma and Christian Life* magazine noted that the Word of Faith teaching was prominent in "most of the new independent black churches, many of which were founded by graduates of Hagin's Rhema Bible Training Center." But their interpretation of Hagin's message often went beyond an emphasis on individual health and prosperity and focused on prosperity, broadly defined, for black communities. In addition, many ministers emphasized conservative "family values," a popular political topic at century's end, as well as racism, social activism, and evangelism. Independent ministers used the faith message to attract African Americans to their churches, offering them hope for the future and building up their individual and communal self-esteem. One minister remarked, "I think that for any black pastor . . . one of the main emphases must be to help believers recognize that they are somebody, they are the righteousness of God, and they don't have to feel inferior. So I teach people how to dream again, how to believe in themselves, how to hope again because of the Word of God."[19] This positive-attitude message resonated deeply with Americans of all racial, ethnic, regional, and socioeconomic backgrounds.

If Kenneth E. Hagin was the father of the modern faith movement, then his spiritual son among African Americans was Frederick K. C. Price.

Price and his wife, Betty, had been Christians for several years, but they struggled financially and with their faith until Price claimed to have received the gift of the Holy Spirit in 1970. Shortly thereafter he was introduced to Hagin's Word of Faith theology. After reading three of his books, Price met Hagin in Albuquerque, New Mexico, and asked his crusade manager if Hagin would preach at his small California church in 1972. A dozen years later Price joked: "I am Brother Hagin's black child . . . and I am proud to be. One of the most beautiful things about [Hagin's] ministry is that it has a world outreach. It also has reached the black community here in the United States. I think it's beautiful what God has done in a very quiet way through this man, his faithfulness, his love, and his generosity of heart in sharing the Word of God. I took that Word of God and in 10 years we've grown from 300 people to 13,230 people at Crenshaw Christian Center in Inglewood, California." Betty Price echoed her husband's sentiments about Hagin's influence on their lives and ministry, and she provided a glimpse into the racial implications of their relationship with Hagin: "I remember when we [first came to Hagin's Campmeeting] in 1973, there was not another black person in the conference. . . . And our hearts went out to our black people. It's like Israel—my heart's desire is that *my* people be saved and *my* people get the Word." Through their television ministry and pastorate of Crenshaw Christian Center, this desire to minister to black Americans was realized. "It's a church of all races," said Betty, "but, naturally, with our being black, we draw more black people."[20]

Fred Price's social activism in the Watts district of Los Angeles, his influence on other Word of Faith ministers, and his popular television teaching ministry made him an important figure in the charismatic movement in his own right. In the late 1970s he even touched the life of football legend Rosie Grier, who joined Price's church and became a proponent of positive confession.[21] Price maintained a close relationship with Hagin's ministry until a controversy over race erupted in the early 1990s that drove a wedge between the two families.[22]

In 1992, at the Rhema Bible Church in Tulsa, Oklahoma, Kenneth Hagin Jr. preached a sermon about interracial dating and marriage. Although he emphatically denied being racist, he argued that if parents did not want their children dating members of different races then they should teach those values at an early age. "I can't tell your kids who to go with and who not to go date," Hagin reportedly stated. "Not my responsibility." He continued: "If you don't want your kids dating somebody, then you control it. But you control it a long time before they ever get to be dating age." He maintained that Christian parents could choose to allow their children to practice interracial dating, but he assured them that they were not racist if they chose otherwise.[23] When a group of black ministers informed Price of Hagin's sermon, Price confronted his friend and asked him to recant his views publicly. Hagin apologized to Price privately and publicly, but Price was not satisfied with a simple apology; he wanted Hagin to renounce those views and take a public stance against racism.[24] Convinced that this issue needed to be addressed, Price preached a yearlong series of televised sermons titled "Race, Religion, and Racism," which became a two-volume book condemning racism in the church.[25]

Price argued that Hagin's views reflected the racist attitudes held by many whites, and that the church needed to speak out against the latent racism ingrained in American society, especially in the American South. "This minister," Price retorted, "is instructing his congregation to teach their children before the children reach dating age. Many white people, especially southern Whites, have trained their children this way. Racism is not in the genes, it starts in the home."[26] He emphasized that he did not think all white people were racist, and he acknowledged that some blacks had developed a "reactive racism" toward whites. This reactive racism, Price proclaimed, helped blacks "keep their sanity in the face of the racist actions and attitudes black people are confronted with on a daily basis," but their racism, while understandable to Price, was not justified.[27] For him the issue was not about interracial dating and marriage, but about the underlying assumption that blacks were inferior to whites, which for some served to justify the position that the two races should not intermingle.[28]

Price wanted to use this incident as a catalyst to launch a movement for change in the church and American society. "I am not angry with any individual person," he insisted, "but I am angry about a situation that until now, apparently, nobody has fully addressed." He characterized his anger as a "holy, righteous indignation" that arose not because his longtime friend hurt his feelings, but because the church—and the nation—still had not effectively dealt with the problem of racism.[29] "I am dealing with a symptom here, not the man," Price contended. "But he represents something. When you are a leader you stand in the pulpit and minister to people, people are going to believe that what you say is from God. That is how racism in America became the mess it is today, because of so-called leaders and ministers talking in this way. Nobody has challenged them. That day is over."[30] Price asserted that slavery was practiced in America for almost three hundred years because the church refused to take a stand against it. He further argued that after emancipation the church continued its "ostrich syndrome, hiding its head in the sand" and refusing to correct the ills that persisted in American society.[31] Price's assault on these attitudes and practices made him a controversial figure, but he continued to influence the development of the charismatic movement at century's end.[32]

In accordance with their long-standing policy not to respond publicly to criticism, the Hagins said little about the controversy, but, according to *Charisma* magazine, Kenneth Hagin Jr. did respond to Rhema supporters privately. He assured them that he tried to apologize to Price personally for the offense and to his church for any hard feelings his statements may have caused. He pointed out that there were interracial couples in his church that remained loyal to him, that he performed wedding ceremonies for mature couples regardless of their race, that key members of his pastoral staff were black, and that many prominent Word of Faith ministers were black. "If people would just take a look at the fruit of this ministry and would talk to people who know me . . . they would understand that I am definitely not a racist, nor am I a bigot in any way," he wrote in a letter to his supporters. "If I could take the words back, I would . . . but I can't. I can only apologize for having said them and pray that the hurt and confusion will be healed."[33] Before and after the controversy, the Hagins consistently featured black speakers at their popular Campmeeting revivals held every year in Tulsa.

Hagin never fully explained why he refused to recant his position, but he continued to react to Price by issuing a veiled call for peace and unity among charismatics in general and the Word of Faith camp in particular. Although neither Price nor the controversial incident was ever mentioned, three articles appeared in his *Word of Faith* magazine in 1998 and 2001 suggesting that Hagin desperately wanted to put the situation behind him. In one article he maintained that Christians could effectively spread the gospel only when they had unity of purpose and did not publicly criticize the mistakes of others. "When conflicts arise," he remarked, "you can either take the low road or the high road. You can take the low road and wallow in the mire, allowing bad feelings or offenses to pull you down. Or you can take the high road and rise up, living above the situation."[34] He continued: "You can choose to dwell on the hurtful things that others have done or said . . . [o]r you can hide God's words inside your heart until they become a part of your mind as well. And when somebody does you wrong, out comes love and forgiveness."[35] Although this incident created a breach between these important pillars of the Word of Faith camp—and caused considerable embarrassment for the younger Hagin—it did not seem to hurt the influence that his ministry had on the charismatic movement.

African Americans continued to support Hagin, and prominent black ministers continued to speak at Campmeetings and other functions sponsored by Kenneth Hagin Ministries. Keith Butler, a 1978 graduate of Rhema Bible Training Center (RBTC), established the Word of Faith Christian Center in Southfield, Michigan, which in 1979 had about 150 members. By the end of the twentieth century his congregation had over 18,000 members; he had a dozen satellite churches located in the United States and its territories; he was a successful Detroit politician; and he had thriving radio, television, and crusade ministries. In 1997 he received a special offering at Hagin's Winter Bible Seminar for RBTC's new media center, and he testified to the influence that the Word of Faith teaching had on his personal and professional life. "My wife and I started our church in a little recreation center with ten people," he remarked. "When we'd come to Tulsa for Campmeeting or other meetings, we'd always bring a special offering from our church, and we would increase the amount of the offering every year. Every time we sowed seed into the special offering, God would give us a miracle, such as a building or equipment that we needed."[36] Butler remained faithful to his friend and mentor despite the public split between the Hagins and Price, and his support helped heal some of the wounds in the Word of Faith movement that were caused by the disagreement over interracial marriage.

Another Word of Faith preacher who gained some prominence in the 1990s was Louisiana native Leroy Thompson. Thompson preached for a Baptist church until he accepted the charismata in 1983 and went to California to study positive confession theology with Fred Price. Price introduced him to Hagin in the mid-1980s, and Thompson began attending Hagin's meetings. He was invited to speak briefly at Campmeeting 1993, and Hagin invited him back as a featured speaker the following year. He continued to work closely with Hagin throughout the 1990s as he built a large television ministry, pastored a congregation of almost two thousand members, and was a featured speaker at many large crusades held by himself and other prominent Word of Faith ministers.[37]

Although there was little formal contact between the two ministers, Creflo Dollar credited Hagin with influencing his ministry as well. Dollar was firmly rooted in the Word of Faith theology, and he taught a self-help gospel that encouraged an entrepreneurial spirit among his upwardly mobile African American audience. Early in his career he immersed himself in the teachings of Kenneth Hagin, Kenneth Copeland, and Oral Roberts, from whom he learned how to organize his ministry and broaden his appeal. According to ministry reports, Dollar held the first service of his World Changers Church International in an Atlanta-area elementary school cafeteria in 1986 with eight people in attendance. He hoped the congregation would grow to five hundred members within a couple of weeks, but it took almost three years to reach that goal and move into a permanent facility. In 1991 he broke ground on a $17 million auditorium called the World Dome, gradually paying for it as he acquired the cash.[38] It was not an easy project, as neighborhood groups and the county government often opposed the church's expansion. But Dollar finally moved into the 8,500-seat structure in 1995. He had by then gained some notoriety in the charismatic world, and his church and ministry grew at a phenomenal rate.[39]

Dollar's message, like that of other charismatic evangelists, claimed to offer hope to hurting people. What made Dollar successful was his ability to apply Hagin's Word of Faith message to the issues that seemed most important to his audience. As African Americans continued moving into the middle class in the 1980s and 1990s, he focused on prosperity, family values, and developing an entrepreneurial spirit that promised personal success. At the beginning of the new millennium, Dollar was poised to become one of the most influential leaders in the charismatic movement in general and the Word of Faith camp in particular.

To a lesser extent, Kenneth E. Hagin also influenced several women evangelists. His protégé, Vicki Jamison-Peterson, had a moderately successful ministry in the 1970s and early 1980s. Raised a pentecostal, she had a "conversion experience" and reportedly spoke in tongues as a child, but she was never completely satisfied with her Christian life. According to her personal testimony, her religious life was "dull and boring"; she even lost her desire to live until she was "miraculously" healed from what doctors thought was cancer. Soon thereafter, she sought the counsel of an "old prophetess" who in 1966 introduced her to Hagin's teachings. "Within three months I was in one of his meetings," she recalled. "He came to speak at the Voice of Healing ministry (now known as Christ for the Nations) . . . taught on his theme Scripture verse, Mark 11:23, and suddenly there was a spiritual explosion inside me."[40] That experience led her to share his positive-attitude, Word of Faith message with her family and friends, and it instilled in her the joy that was lacking in her life.

Jamison-Peterson attended a charismatic Bible institute in Dallas, Texas, before joining Hagin in 1971 as a singer at his crusades.[41] She and her husband traveled with Hagin for a year and a half before she was hospitalized with internal bleeding in 1972. The doctors were unable to stop her from hemorrhaging and had lost hope for her survival. Unwilling to give up, Jamison-Peterson employed the positive-confession techniques she learned from Hagin and within thirty minutes the bleeding had reportedly stopped. "From time to time the symptoms of the affliction try to come back upon me, trying to tell me I'm going to die," she later confessed. "But every time I stand upon the Word of God . . . I declare, 'I am healed by God's power.' And the symptoms have always disappeared."[42] Her confidence in Hagin's Word of Faith message was prevalent in her own teaching and contributed to her modest success.

Another important, although less popular, figure was Billye Brim. A former Baptist, Brim attended some of Hagin's Tulsa revival meetings, where in 1967 she accepted the charismata. Her conversion led to a close association with Hagin; from 1971 until 1980 Brim edited Hagin's sermons into books and articles for his *Word of Faith* magazine. During that time she was active in her local congregation in Collinsville, Oklahoma, taught a few classes at RBTC, and occasionally preached at revival meetings on weekends. She was also a housewife and mother of four. Brim reported that some time in the 1970s, while standing at her kitchen sink peeling potatoes for supper, she received a revelation that she was to focus her future ministry on the role that Jews would play in biblical prophecy. In 1980 she resigned from Kenneth Hagin Ministries to become a full-time evangelist.[43] Although she did not have the media exposure or name recognition that other charismatic evangelists had, she had gained some notoriety by the turn of the century. She embodied the traits of the modern charismatic woman—successful wife, mother, businessperson, and evangelist—and she owed much of her success to Hagin and his teachings.

Lynette Hagin, Kenneth Hagin Jr.'s wife, was also an important part of this ministry. Her husband began his career as a youth minister and then as associate pastor at her father's church. Hagin had been preaching regularly at his father-in-law's church when his father, Kenneth E. Hagin, asked him to become his crusade director. Lynette and Kenneth Jr.'s salary was cut in half, he was removed from the spotlight, and his responsibilities ranged from counting the offerings to setting up book displays to catching people as they were "slain in the Spirit" in his father's healing lines. Early in their marriage Lynette focused much of her attention on raising her children, until she became director of RBTC in May of 1982. Even then, she mainly served "behind the scenes" in an administrative capacity, and she seemed most interested in ministering to women in a more "traditional" sense. In the late 1990s she assumed more public roles in the ministry, but she did not try to elevate her level of public involvement to that of other wives of prominent evangelists. One of the first articles she wrote for the *Word of Faith* magazine appeared in 1998, and in 2001 she sponsored a women's conference at Rhema Bible Church, which included, among others, herself, her daughter Denise Hagin Burns, and her daughter-in-law Melissa Robertson Hagin as featured speakers.[44] This type of family involvement provided a sense of stability and continuity in the Hagin ministry, which contributed to its solidification and growth.

Growth of Kenneth Hagin Ministries

Radio and print media were central to Hagin's outreach from the beginning. Freda Lindsay of the Voice of Healing ministry persuaded him to publish his first book in 1960, and she and her staff edited his books for several years thereafter. In the mid-1960s Gordon Lindsay asked Hagin to teach on his radio show in Dallas, which offered added exposure. Hagin moved his ministry headquarters from Texas to Tulsa, Oklahoma, in 1966, expanded his tape ministry, and began his own radio program called *Faith Seminar of the Air.* In 1968 he started sending a regular newsletter to his supporters, which later became the *Word of Faith* magazine. His popularity grew after 1967, but he kept his ministry small; in 1973 he had only nineteen full-time employees. He continued to conduct meetings and seminars in hotels and churches around the country, and in the summer of 1973 he held his first annual Campmeeting at a Tulsa church with over four hundred people in attendance. By 1976 it had become so large that he moved it to the Tulsa Convention Center, and by 1982 his crowds had reportedly grown to as many as 24,000. At century's end, the Campmeeting's popularity had declined somewhat, with attendance dipping to about 12,000 in 1998 and only 8,000 in 2000, but it was still popular among the Word of Faith faithful.

Hagin continued in his role as teacher when he branched out into television in 1976 with *The Faith That Lives* program, but his mainstay continued to be radio broadcasts, sales of sermon tapes, and print media. By 1981 he and his son, Kenneth Hagin Jr., had written eighty-five books, and their magazine reportedly went to 160,000 homes. By the year 2000,

Kenneth Hagin Ministries had grown considerably. The ministry claimed that his radio show was heard on over three hundred daily American broadcasts and in 120 foreign countries. It also claimed that Hagin and his son had written 130 books and sold 60 million copies; the *Word of Faith* magazine had a circulation of over half a million; and the ministry distributed over 58,000 tapes each month. The staff had also grown to nearly three hundred employees.[45]

Probably the most enduring aspect of Hagin's ministry was the founding of Rhema Bible Training Center in 1974, which allowed his ministry to solidify, institutionalize, and spread his faith message all over the world. It started as a one-year program with only fifty-eight students; by 2001 it offered two- and three-year programs and had an average annual enrollment of 1,700 students. RBTC was designed to teach the practical applications of ministry and prepare men and women for full-time church work. Hagin believed that the charismatic movement in general did not emphasize Bible study enough, and he wanted to provide training for a large number of charismatics who wanted to serve in the ministry but did not have the requisite skills to do so. He did not intend to compete with liberal arts universities, such as Oral Roberts University, or small Bible colleges and institutes, such as Gordon and Freda Lindsay's Christ for the Nations International, which had become important institutions for many evangelicals.[46]

Hagin created an impressive network of Rhema graduates and cultivated it through persistent communication via magazines, newsletters, the Internet, and seminars. The Rhema Ministerial Association International (RMAI) provided a spiritual network that, according to Hagin, would increase world evangelization and hasten the second coming of Christ.[47] David Beebe, Alumni Association director in 2001, reported that the Rhema Supportive Ministries Association was created "to recognize, encourage, help, train, and *connect* our alumni as they do their part in this last great harvest for the Kingdom of God." Like many other educational institutions, RBTC created a website so alumni could "stay *connected* to your classmates and access updated information about RBTC and its graduates."[48]

Furthermore, RBTC established satellite schools throughout the world in the 1980s and 1990s, allowing Hagin to increase his influence in the burgeoning overseas charismatic movement. By 2001 fourteen foreign schools were formally affiliated with Rhema USA. These schools were established partly to minimize the number of international students who chose not to return to their native countries after living in America. Addressing this issue, Kenneth Hagin Jr. stated: "Many workers from developing nations who had come to the United States for training became westernized and didn't want to return to villages where they may have fewer modern conveniences. But establishing RHEMA Bible Training Centers in or near their homelands could minimize that situation."[49] These schools also provided Hagin with a level of name recognition that he would not have otherwise received.

New York Times reporter Norimitsu Onishi noticed the impact that Hagin's ministry and prosperity message had in Nigeria. The number of pentecostal and charismatic churches increased dramatically in the 1990s—from 50 to 250 according to the Pentecostal Fellowship Movement of Nigeria. Men and women who were influenced by Hagin's Word of Faith message led many of these churches. David Oyedepo, for example, founded the Winner's Church in Lagos, Nigeria, in 1989. Ten years later he moved his operation to "a 565-acre walled campus with a hotel, gas station, bank, restaurants, shops, the foundation of a university and the continent's largest church auditorium" in Otto, Nigeria. He claimed to have modeled his ministry on that of Kenneth Hagin, and he "waved away the possibility that any social and economic reasons might lie behind the boom in Pentecostal churches, saying only, 'It's a divine time'" for African charismatics.[50]

Former Nigerian pop singer Chris Okotie also studied at RBTC; he founded the Household of God church in 1987. He moved into a warehouse in 1993 and then bought an entire block—twenty acres—of warehouses, a 1,500-car parking lot, and began construction on a six-story school to accommodate his ministry. In a country where nearly one-third of its population made less than one dollar a day and about 40 percent were illiterate, Okotie drove a new black Mercedes-Benz, hired several bodyguards for protection, and had an elaborate security system for the church grounds. In a pamphlet for new members, Oyedepo summed up the importance of the prosperity message to the success of his and Okotie's churches: "Prosperity is acknowledged worldwide as the identity of our ministry. God prospers here. He will prosper you too!" This celebration of wealth resonated deeply with the impoverished Nigerian population.[51]

Another milestone in the success of Kenneth Hagin Ministries was the establishment of Rhema Bible Church on the RBTC campus. It began a full schedule of services in 1985 with Kenneth Hagin Jr. serving as senior pastor, and it had nearly 7,000 members by 1995. The church served as a support base for Kenneth Hagin Ministries and RBTC, providing training and practical ministerial experience for Rhema students. The establishment of satellite churches and a ministerial fellowship also contributed to the growth of the Word of Faith message and the Hagins' influence worldwide. Kenneth E. Hagin's grandchildren, Craig and Denise, joined the church staff in the 1990s.[52] Craig Hagin, born in 1969, was raised around the Hagins' ministry, helping at crusades and working in the groundskeeping and maintenance departments as a teenager. While in high school he decided to enter the ministry, but he and his wife, Melissa, earned business degrees from Oklahoma State University in 1991 before attending RBTC. Craig Hagin began his career in 1991 as special meetings coordinator and operations manager for Kenneth Hagin Ministries. He later became an associate pastor at Rhema Bible Church, and his wife worked as a management assistant to her mother-in-law, Lynette Hagin.[53] Denise Hagin also went on crusades as a child, worked part time at RBTC as a teenager, volunteered at Rhema Bible Church, and "felt called" to the ministry during her senior year in high school. She dabbled in modeling and considered a career in fashion design, but became interested in children's ministry in high school and majored in early childhood education in college. She was appointed full-time preschool director at Rhema Bible Church while still completing her undergraduate degree. She graduated from RBTC in 1998 and served as preschool director at Rhema Bible Church, instructor at RBTC, and children's coordinator for their annual Campmeeting.[54]

Conclusion

Kenneth E. Hagin's contributions to the modern charismatic movement were numerous and lasting. His propagation of the Word of Faith teaching through his books, tapes, magazine, radio and television programs, meetings, and training center made him an important leader in one of the fastest growing religious phenomena in modern American history.[55] A number of scholars have documented how Hagin's teachings spread to other countries and were adapted to various cultural contexts. Many proponents of the faith message attended RBTC or Word of Faith seminars and conferences and then returned to their native lands to propagate the prosperity message. Their ability to adapt it to their specific social, cultural, and economic contexts is a striking testament to the pliability of the theology. Many of these scholars credit Hagin with being the source of the core message, and they acknowledge the influence he had in the spread of the charismatic movement.[56]

The keys to his success were his prosperity message, which offered hope to anyone who wanted a more fulfilling life, and his stable institutions, which produced thousands of people propounding that message. The most impressive growth of the Word of Faith movement came through African American preachers, who carried the prosperity message to black communities throughout the United States and abroad. They adapted and crafted this message to meet the economic, social, emotional, and religious needs of poor and middle-class blacks who were struggling to find their place in the post–civil rights era. In the process they, like other religious entrepreneurs in American history, created for themselves important and often lucrative religious empires. Unlike Oral Roberts, Hagin's influence on the charismatic movement was subtle and felt only with the passage of time, but his contributions to its growth—especially among African Americans—were equally important. By the end of the twentieth century, Hagin's faith message had had a profound influence on charismatic thought worldwide, and RBTC had become a stable institution that was well funded, well connected, and well on its way to becoming a loose denomination. Hagin succeeded because he adopted a simple and popular message, he created institutions that perpetuated his message, and he continued to shape that message and those institutions until his death in 2003.

6
Rock Fights, Quarantines, and Confessionals
B. C. Goodpasture, the *Gospel Advocate*, and Keeping Order in Churches of Christ

John C. Hardin

On Sunday, January 8, 1950, the *New York Times* carried a front-page story about the stoning of American missionaries in Italy. The missionaries, thirteen in all, arrived in Italy in January 1949 under the sponsorship of the Crescent Hill Church of Christ in Brownfield, Texas. Operating on temporary visas, they preached in towns near Rome, established an orphanage at Frascati, and distributed aid of various kinds. But their attempts to proselytize native Italians in an overwhelmingly Roman Catholic country met with violence. Crowds threw stones at the missionaries in four towns, succeeding at driving them out in each instance, albeit uninjured. A more daring group of local residents dynamited a Jeep belonging to the orphanage. Others physically harassed some of the more than two hundred converts gained by the Americans. The last stoning incident in 1949 took place in December at Castel Gandolfo, the location of the papal summer residence, and press reports in the United States followed soon thereafter. The missionaries claimed that Catholic priests had incited young parishioners against them, and they accused the Italian government of agreeing to Catholic demands to deny them permanent visas, stop their distribution of aid packages, and close their orphanage.[1]

Many members of Churches of Christ, especially in Texas, expressed outrage with the Italian government and the Roman Catholic Church for their treatment of the missionaries. Imploring the American government to address the situation, they formed committees, drafted resolutions, held rallies in Dallas and Houston, wrote congressional representatives, appealed to the State Department, and sent a mass telegram to President Truman. Publicity in the national press continued, which, in addition to intensifying the indignation, brought out a certain amount of denominational pride and optimism. On the front page of the influential *Gospel Advocate,* published weekly in Nashville, prominent Texas preacher M. Norvel Young wrote, "Evidently more people have heard of the churches of Christ through this means than any such event in our generation. The most widely-read news magazines are carrying stories on it."[2]

Other church members, however, considered the overt denominational response to the reports in Italy a disappointing and alarming departure from historic practice. Churches of Christ had long prided themselves on their undenominational identity, which was rooted in strict adherence to congregational autonomy and aversion to intercongregational cooperation. Cled E. Wallace, a staff writer for the Texas-based *Gospel Guardian,* satirized the entire episode in a front-page article, "That Rock Fight in Italy." His disparagement of both the protestors and the missionaries created a firestorm of controversy.

Criticizing the denominational reaction of supposedly undenominational Christians, he remarked, "Maybe if we keep our shirts on and our hats on straight, 'our' denomination may be able to appoint enough committees and draft enough resolutions to influence the pope to call off his rock throwing." Later defining "denomination" for his readers, Wallace gave expression to an anti-institutional mindset that in years past had been more prevalent among Churches of Christ: "A denomination, as commonly accepted, is something in the way of a religious organization, which is smaller than the 'church in the universal sense' and larger than 'a local congregation.' There isn't anything like it in the New Testament. This 'mass-meeting' in Dallas certainly cannot qualify as 'the church in a universal sense' nor as 'a local congregation.'"[3]

Benton Cordell Goodpasture, editor of the *Gospel Advocate,* typified the kind of denominational consciousness that Wallace found distasteful. Warning of "the encroachments of Romanism in this country," Goodpasture decried "the outrageous treatment of our brethren in Italy." He praised those "who have gone to Rome to preach the gospel in that priest-ridden and benighted city [and who] have manifested a Pauline courage." His response to Wallace was representative of many others: "If the stoning of these young men in Italy by a Romish mob may be dubbed a 'rock fight,' then may we think of Paul as having been 'knocked out' and Stephen as having been killed in a 'rock fight'? . . . We prefer to sympathize with these brethren and pray for them rather than ridicule them in their persecution by dubbing their afflictions a 'rock fight.'"[4] Hostile responses of that sort caught Wallace off guard, but they should not have.

Rapid growth and change had recently come to Churches of Christ, and as a result old and new attitudes were uneasily coexisting at the outset of what would prove to be a very eventful decade.

Informal Authority

Originating in the first decade of the nineteenth century, the American restoration movement, often called the Stone-Campbell movement, began to blossom in the 1820s and 1830s, and so did its papers and editors.[5] Alexander Campbell's *Christian Baptist* (1823–30) and *Millennial Harbinger* (1830–70), Barton Stone's *Christian Messenger* (1826–45), and Walter Scott's *Evangelist* (1832–42) defined the movement in its first generation. More papers and more editors defined subsequent generations. Without a formal power structure in the movement, some editors became what various observers have called "editor-bishops." According to historian Richard T. Hughes, the "people in the pews voted for these 'bishops' with their subscriptions," consequently bestowing great influence upon them.[6] Churches of Christ emerged as a distinct group within the movement after the Civil War, and several movement leaders started papers that reflected the conservative nature of the group. The *Gospel Advocate,* founded in 1855 in Nashville and edited for five decades by David Lipscomb, became the most influential of those papers and defined Churches of Christ more than any other.

The *Advocate* spoke primarily for highly sectarian and fiercely autonomous southern churches populated by men and women intent on following the proper New Testament "pattern" of work and worship. These Christians also had a strong otherworldly focus. They tended to be poor in earthly possessions and influence, but rich in fervor for serving God and his kingdom. Their "cultural separatism," according to David Edwin Harrell Jr., was rooted in both "social and intellectual discontent." As the decades passed, however, Churches of Christ changed. During the World War II era, especially, they grew rapidly in size, wealth, education, and influence. Consequently, the sense of alienation—whether social or cultural, intellectual or theological—diminished just as rapidly for many church members. "By the 1950s," Harrell observed, "churches were filled with upwardly mobile, successful Americans who yearned for recognition for themselves and their church. They built their denomination, they advertised their successes, and they set out to prove to their fellow Americans that they were worthy of a place under the canopy of America's patriotic civil religion."[7] But not all was well. Church members who still disdained "modernizing schemes, institutional structures, and denominational standing" reacted vigorously against the new attitude.[8]

In March 1939, with Churches of Christ in the midst of transition, B. C. Goodpasture, an Atlanta preacher and Tennessee native, became editor of the *Gospel Advocate.* He brought with him to Nashville the image of respectability that many in Churches of Christ wanted to project. As *Advocate* editor until his death in 1977, he provided leadership to Churches of Christ in several ways, but two were primary. First, he gradually built affiliations with progressive preachers, churches, and institutions, and participated with them in a spirit of boosterism that emerged after World War II and accelerated in the 1950s, topping out by the late 1960s. In short, he saw to it that the *Advocate* thoroughly promoted the interests, activities, and institutions of Churches of Christ in any way that it could, thereby contributing to their organization, group identity, and significant postwar growth. Those who affiliated with Goodpasture were not theological liberals, but were progressive in the sense of being open to contemporary attitudes and methods. Increasingly educated and engaged with the broader culture, they were intent on doing "big" things, and doing them in a way that not only brought souls to Christ but also moved Churches of Christ into the mainstream of respectable society.

Second, having emerged at the center of a network of progressive leaders and institutions by 1950, Goodpasture wielded his accumulated power to help bring coherence to Churches of Christ and maintain unity in the face of an anti-institutional backlash. His role in the postwar institutional debate was to keep order in Churches of Christ—to maintain a rapidly crystallizing consensus on matters of doctrine, method, and sensibility in order to stay "on the march." Maintaining consensus meant not only rallying the troops but also dealing with dissenters. Thus, in the mid-1950s, Goodpasture and other leaders launched an offensive intended to discredit and isolate those who assailed the majority view. Goodpasture executed his role well, and his success defined his legacy, for good or ill, among Churches of Christ.

In recent times, historians have written about the survival of American fundamentalism in the 1930s and 1940s after it largely passed from the public eye as a disgraced national movement in the late 1920s.[9] While out of the spotlight, fundamentalists retreated and reorganized, informally building regional institutional networks that allowed their doctrines and zeal to thrive at the grassroots level. William Bell Riley, for instance, was one fundamentalist who headed an informal regional network in the Midwest. In his study of Riley, William Vance Trollinger Jr. emphasized the central importance of parachurch institutions such as papers and schools, as well as powerful personalities, to the establishment and maintenance of networks like the one built by Riley. From his large and visible Baptist church in Minneapolis, Riley directed his "empire," which had its beginnings early in the century with the founding of his Northwestern Bible and Missionary Training School. Through that school and his monthly paper, Riley instilled a vast number of ministers and lay Christians with fundamentalist doctrine and missionary zeal. He placed ministers all over the Midwest and kept close tabs on them to make sure they did not depart from the orthodoxy he taught them. The Northwestern school and its trappings essentially became a denominational surrogate for many individuals and churches in the Midwest. Due in large part to networks like Riley's, by 1950 neo-fundamentalism had begun to emerge at a national level, notably represented by evangelists like Billy Graham and organizations such as Youth for Christ.[10]

Informal networks of schools, papers, and ministers, then, were crucial to sustaining fundamentalism. Among the similarly unstructured Churches of Christ, such networks proved equally vital. Often with powerful personalities at the center, they promoted group identity, defined and enforced doctrinal orthodoxy, contributed to growth and unity, delineated division, and bound individuals and congregations to one another. Historian Douglas A. Foster, writing as an insider, has remarked on the informal "structures that served to hold us together and give us an identity." According to Foster, "Sometimes those informal structures have wielded as much power as any official denominational organization." In particular, schools, lectureships, and papers, as "the major centers of influence and power in Churches of Christ," have been "institutions of control and uniformity." In fact, "these institutions usually worked together to create and maintain a consensus on everything from the order and time of worship to positions on theological matters. . . . Together, they exerted a powerful influence on this group of autonomous congregations, making us amazingly uniform. Those who did not agree with the positions they defined were often excluded from fellowship through the workings of the same institutions."[11] As editor of the *Gospel Advocate,* B. C. Goodpasture headed an institution that, according to David Harrell, was "the most powerful single center of influence among the churches of Christ of the 1950s."[12] He thus possessed significant informal authority at a particularly important time for Churches of Christ, and his skillful use of that authority meant that the *Advocate* "wielded as much power as any official denominational organization."[13]

To the Top

When the *Gospel Advocate* editorship became vacant in January 1938, several influential church leaders contacted publisher Leon B. McQuiddy to express their opinions about filling the position. Among progressives, the sentiment expressed by Jesse P. Sewell, former president of Abilene Christian College in Texas, was typical. Sewell considered McQuiddy's task a "grave responsibility." He wrote to McQuiddy several times, inundating him with unsolicited advice and the names of acceptable candidates for the job. Anticipating that the next editor would provide crucial direction for Churches of Christ during a time of transition, Sewell implored McQuiddy to hire someone who would provide "constructive leadership" to "the churches and individual Christians." They needed "sane" leadership now more than ever. The *Advocate,* he advised, "constitutes a center of influence and leadership among a large group of disciples which is all but absolute. The way it goes in spirit, attitude, teaching and character this large group goes and will go." To Sewell, it was imperative that McQuiddy heed his counsel.[14]

After many months of weighing his options, McQuiddy offered the position to Goodpasture, who—incidentally or not—seemed to meet Sewell's criteria. Goodpasture, though, not sure that he was fit for the job, was reluctant to accept the weighty responsibility of the *Advocate* editorship. But his mentor, senior *Advocate* staff writer H. Leo Boles, who pushed McQuiddy to hire Goodpasture, urged his forty-three-year-old protégé to put aside his misgivings and take the job at once. "The present opportunity," he wrote, "is a golden opportunity for you; it gives you opportunity to rise 'to the top' in the brotherhood, and places you in [a] position [that] many are now aspiring to reach." Moreover, Boles feared that if Goodpasture did not accept the offer, McQuiddy might turn to someone with a "fighting style," someone like Texas firebrand Foy E. Wallace Jr., who edited the *Advocate* from 1930 to 1934. Boles declared to Goodpasture that he "would regret exceedingly to see 'the ark of God fall into the hands of the Philistines.' . . . No one in the brotherhood is better qualified for this place than you. You just must accept the proposition." One can imagine Boles's relief and elation when, in January 1939, Goodpasture finally agreed to edit the *Advocate.*[15]

Initially, Goodpasture experienced a generally positive reception, but sharp criticism came soon enough. Some detractors suspected that he was "soft" doctrinally, and they resented his refusal to publish articles by certain outspoken conservatives. Foy Wallace, as editor of the upstart *Bible Banner*, was in the forefront of this criticism throughout the 1940s. But he was not alone. Particularly severe was the criticism of one of Goodpasture's former staff writers, R. L. Whiteside, who left the *Advocate* to write for the *Banner*. Among other grievances, Whiteside detested Goodpasture's treatment of Wallace. Goodpasture and others sometimes responded to Wallace with personal attacks that were "full of venom," as Whiteside put it. Lamenting the paper that he had supported for more than fifty years, Whiteside declared, "How has the once great and mighty *Advocate* fallen! It pains me more than I can express that such miserable drink flows through the *Advocate* that I have loved all these years. It is nauseating." Later, when trying to understand the hold Goodpasture seemed to have on some people, Whiteside indirectly commented on the informal political power of the *Advocate:* "Some likely do not try to correct the editor, fearing they will lose the favor of the editor." Nevertheless, "the man who will shut his eyes against wrong and kow-tow to men who he thinks are in position to grant him favors is a sorry specimen of manhood."[16]

One person Whiteside might have had in mind when he made that statement was Price Billingsley, a Texas preacher. Billingsley was antagonistic toward Goodpasture from the beginning of his editorship, but soon changed his attitude. Publicly calling Goodpasture "a panty-waist editor" in 1939, he wrote to him privately in 1942 to complain of the *Advocate*'s endorsement of A. R. Holton, a Nashville preacher. Billingsley, who did not consider Holton "a true gospel preacher," informed Goodpasture, "It is just such announcements . . . which deeply discourages the faithful of the Lord in what the Advocate stands for." Billingsley did not expect his opinion to "[mean] one thing to the unworthy successor of the once-noble line of Gospel Advocate editors," nor did he "hope ever to see much good come from [Goodpasture's] pip-squeak voice." But just four years later, in 1946, Billingsley took a markedly different stance. In a letter to Goodpasture, he wrote, "Your facility to write and your unalterable stand for New Testament truth deeply gratify me. I feel increasing delight in your editorials, [and] feel that for the years ahead, the welfare of the cause of the Lord is eminently safe in your hands." Three months later, retired but in need of income, Billingsley asked Goodpasture and McQuiddy for a job. From that point forward he remained a solid friend of the *Advocate*.[17]

Unlike Billingsley, other preachers were in step with Goodpasture from the very beginning of his editorship. One striking example was G. C. Brewer, an outspoken progressive preacher of great prominence. When Goodpasture became editor, Brewer began courting his favor, hoping once again to grace the pages of the *Advocate* after being shut out for several years. He was eager, as he explained to Goodpasture, "to put the brethren right in regard to me and my teaching." Ever since the early 1930s, when Foy Wallace had used the *Advocate* to declare him "unsound," there had been "a decrease in the things" coming to him. Wanting Goodpasture to allow him "the opportunity of getting back," Brewer made a request of the editor: "I want to write a number of articles on very basic and fundamental principles, and I want to appear in the Gospel Advocate *every week* for at least eight, ten, or twelve weeks. . . . There is no reason why my writing should not be as widely read again, or that my discussion of points might not be as much in demand." Not surprisingly, Brewer would become one of Goodpasture's key allies.[18]

Gospel Guardian

Brewer, in fact, was one of a handful of writers in the 1940s and '50s who served particularly crucial roles for Goodpasture, helping him push specific points of view and do battle with foes both within Churches of Christ and without. The most significant of the internal battles in this period was the institutional controversy. It revolved around two related issues: (1) the degree to which congregations could scripturally cooperate with one another, and (2) the proper relationship of congregations to church-related institutions. In the first case, the controversy initially concerned mission works, and later included media ventures. In the second case, the turmoil centered on colleges and schools, and then expanded to orphanages and other benevolent institutions. These issues were not completely new, but large-scale efforts to fund colleges and postwar missions brought them to the fore by the end of the 1940s. In a fellowship that required biblical authority for all aspects of church work and worship, and which placed great value on congregational autonomy, and which shunned denominational behavior, these were questions of great import.

A central phase of the institutional controversy began in May 1949 with the first issue of the *Gospel Guardian*. Published in Lufkin, Texas, by Roy E. Cogdill, and edited by Fanning Yater Tant, the paper was a continuation of Foy Wallace's *Bible Banner*. In the last issue of the *Banner*, Tant declared the intention of the *Guardian* to combat institutionalism and other "apostacies" in a "militant and aggressive" manner. "We are unalterably opposed to the unscriptural idea of having the college supported out of the church treasury," he wrote, "[and] we view with considerable apprehension the apparent drift toward an 'institutional conscious' missionary program—the feeling that we cannot preach the gospel without an elaborate institutional set-up." The *Guardian* thus represented a serious challenge to institutional leaders. Goodpasture and many others were convinced that the noninstitutional viewpoint represented by the *Guardian* was extreme, and if allowed to increase in favor would endanger everything Churches of Christ had gained in previous decades. N. B. Hardeman, a revered preacher and longtime president of Freed-Hardeman College in west Tennessee, expressed his worries in a letter to an ailing Goodpasture: "I can't help but have some fears regarding the Advocate. I have read the Gospel Guardian's announcement and it seems to me that it is almost largely directed against the Advocate. If you can recover and continue with it, all will be well that long at least."[19]

Goodpasture did recover—perhaps from a severe asthmatic reaction—and soon began attempts at discrediting "those who pose as leaders and guardians of orthodoxy." His initial tact focused on highlighting doctrinal inconsistencies among noninstitutional leaders, while generally avoiding engagement on the issues they raised. "When professed teachers and leaders show such instability," he wrote, "the effect on the rank and file of the church is most disheartening and injurious. It is a bit upsetting for people to be led in one direction for a while, and then discover that their trusted leaders have deserted them and gone in the opposite direction."[20] G. C. Brewer, meanwhile, wrote to Goodpasture to offer his estimation of the *Guardian*: "You said you didn't think the Guardian would succeed, and I don't think so either, but I do know that a great many brethren say that we need the paper if it would be just a little less bitter in its personal attacks." Brewer outlined a plan of action: "It is my opinion that we should hit this thing a death blow. . . . We [should] condemn any effort to create an issue, where no issue has ever before existed, and to start a faction. This is wrong and we should expose the thing and condemn it." Soon thereafter, Brewer published a lengthy article in the *Advocate* that followed his own advice. He argued that the *Guardian* irresponsibly criticized long-standing and defensible practices, thereby creating false issues, and that it represented a divisive minority faction that should "be marked and avoided."[21]

Although Goodpasture, Hardeman, Brewer, and others attempted to portray the *Guardian* and its supporters as troublemakers with narrow concerns, the *Guardian* nevertheless made it clear that the institutional controversy was about more than specific practices. The common threads running through their objections were concerns about "centralization," "institutionalism," and "denominationalism."[22] With the onset of the 1950s, they intensified those objections and increasingly directed them at Goodpasture and the *Advocate.* Cled Wallace's witty but irreverent 1950 "rock fight" article—and his subsequent attempts to clarify it—highlighted the *Guardian*'s concerns about dangerous trends within Churches of Christ. In defending himself, Wallace addressed the sponsoring-church arrangement used to fund the Italian missionaries. Even before the end of World War II, certain large congregations began planning ambitious overseas missionary endeavors. They invited smaller churches with limited resources to contribute funds to the projects through them, the sponsoring churches. This method allowed for great strides in the mission field without resorting to the formation of an independent missionary society, long abhorred by Churches of Christ as unscriptural. Moreover, this funding method did not threaten the autonomy of any congregation since participation was voluntary. That, at least, was the view of proponents of the sponsoring-church method. Cled Wallace voiced a different opinion. "I'm a bit worried," he wrote, referring to the Crescent Hill congregation's sponsorship of the Italian missionaries, "about a church's right to plan a big program that it can't pay for . . . and line up 'contributing churches' to work through 'the sponsoring church.'"[23]

Like Wallace, *Guardian* editor Yater Tant tried to turn the Italian controversy toward scrutiny of the limits of congregational cooperation: "Is there a scriptural precedent for, or an example of, the elders of one 'sponsoring' church becoming the controlling and directing medium through which many other churches may spend their money and discharge their responsibility in a foreign field?" Definitely not, he answered. *Guardian* publisher Roy Cogdill agreed, observing that the sponsoring-church issue boiled down to "whether we follow God's way or follow our own way." Clearly, Cogdill asserted, "God did not provide for any concentration of power in one congregation, but gave the same jurisdiction to all, and made each responsible for its own work. No congregation has the right to delegate that responsibility to another church." Likewise, Cogdill continued, "centralization of power [is not] to be assumed by one congregation." Concerned that the *Guardian* stood "alone" in its opposition to sponsoring-church arrangements, Tant questioned why other papers, including the *Advocate,* did not recognize the "developing" danger. He surmised that they did not understand the "nature of the threat" and that their editors had "a general desire not to rock the boat when things are going well." In particular, the *Advocate*'s growing "popularity" seemed "to blind her eyes to the dangers ahead." At any rate, Tant declared, if some were "set on leading the church into apostasy," the *Guardian* was prepared to lead a "battle . . . waged without restraint," even if it meant that Churches of Christ would suffer "the agony of . . . division."[24]

In the *Advocate,* Goodpasture and others were testy in their response to the *Guardian*'s assault. Cecil N. Wright, a Denver preacher, hoped that the *Guardian*'s talk of division over the issue was "just so much bluster." He could not see how the paper could justify an attack on "the principle of 'sponsored' cooperation," a principle he considered unassailable. G. C. Brewer, like Wright, was dismissive of the *Guardian*'s rant. He proudly pointed out that Churches of Christ "accomplished more in the mission fields" in the five years since World War II than in any other five-year period, "quibblers" like the *Guardian* notwithstanding. Goodpasture, seemingly doing his best to ignore the *Guardian,* ran out of patience when Yater Tant quoted from a 1940 *Advocate* article by his deceased mentor, H. Leo Boles. Tant implied that the *Guardian* merely held the same position on congregational cooperation as the venerable Boles, and that the *Advocate* apparently had drifted from that position. Clearly frustrated, Goodpasture insisted that Tant had "garbled" and made "absurd use" of the Boles article, and reprinted it in full.[25]

On the March

Generally not alarmed by the issues raised by the *Guardian,* 1950s-era progressives kept busily "on the march," a phrase they regularly applied to Churches of Christ. Goodpasture, in fact, employed the metaphor in three editorials in the space of three months in 1952. Exhorting readers to "let our lights shine," he proudly announced that "the brotherhood is on the march." Its "influence . . . for good is being extended and recognized in this generation." He took special delight in citing the positive appraisals of outsiders. Their assessments were "proof that the influence of the churches of Christ is being felt in this country. The churches are awakening to a new sense of responsibility. They are on the march." Goodpasture also found it "gratifying to see the rapid growth of the church in our generation. The hosts of the Lord are bestirring themselves. A mighty army is on the march. The gospel is being preached in the neglected sections of our own country and to the far ends of the earth. May this be only the beginning of a movement that will soon carry the primitive gospel to every creature in the whole world."[26]

Goodpasture's statements captured the euphoria of an expanding church. Like other religious groups in the United States, Churches of Christ experienced rapid growth following the Second World War.[27] Indeed, some believed they were growing the fastest of all. In 1947 there were an estimated 680,000 church members in 10,000 congregations, conservative figures that alone indicated significant gains since the 1920s. By 1960 liberal estimates had the membership figure more than doubling to 2 million. Such estimates were bloated, based more on rosy perceptions than data.[28] Yet whatever its rate, numerical growth was occurring and feeding the group's robust optimism. Moreover, church members gained in education and affluence. As a result, congregations erected modern buildings in highly visible areas; churches sent missionaries to foreign and domestic fields in record numbers; and the oldest Church of Christ colleges gained accreditation, even as church members founded others. Various projects, often of a national scope, indicated that Churches of Christ were intent on making a place for themselves within conservative middle-class American culture, even as they saved souls. Perhaps most important was the establishment of a national radio and television program in the early 1950s, the *Herald of Truth*, produced under the oversight of the Highland Church of Christ in Abilene, Texas. Other cooperative ventures included the creation of the Gospel Press, which raised money to place advertisements in national magazines on behalf of Churches of Christ; a major fund-raising campaign to buy property in the heart of Manhattan so Churches of Christ could establish a respectable and visible presence in "the capital of the world"; and the founding of a new periodical, the *Voice of Freedom*, which trumpeted Americanism and preached anti-Catholicism and anti-Communism to an audience broader than Churches of Christ.[29] In short, postwar Churches of Christ were proud of their Christian commitment and their place in society. It was this denominational pride that was so offended by Wallace's "rock fight" article and revealed in Goodpasture's "on the march" language.

Advocate writers shared this "on the march" attitude. Staff writer Ira North represented the new mindset as well as anyone in the entire fellowship, and he exemplified the kinds of affiliations Goodpasture built among the churches and the colleges. North preached for the large and growing Madison Church of Christ near Nashville, whose guiding slogan the *Ad-*

vocate publicized: "Our Lord thought big, planned big, and commanded big." North, who had a PhD in speech, also served on the faculty of David Lipscomb College in Nashville, which he promoted with as much fervor as he did Madison, the *Advocate,* and Churches of Christ. Author of the aptly titled *You Can March for the Master,* published by the Gospel Advocate Company in 1959, North's writings in the *Advocate* were typically positive. In a characteristic article published in December 1954, North touted the potential of Churches of Christ during the upcoming year. "Probably not since the first century," he wrote, "have there been so many open doors for New Testament Christianity. The future is bright. The church of our Lord is on the march. *Let's be alive in '55!*"[30]

North fully appreciated the fact that Nashville was an ideal location for influencing Churches of Christ. He informed Goodpasture in a 1957 letter that he was not going to pursue another job opportunity recently presented to him. His words simultaneously captured the booster mentality of progressives; the interconnections between the *Advocate,* the colleges, and the churches; and the *Advocate* and its editor as a nexus of influence in Churches of Christ. "I'm taking your advice and staying at Madison, Lipscomb, and with the GA," North wrote. "From Middle Tennessee we have great opportunities to do things for the Cause. With B. C. Goodpasture in the drivers [*sic*] seat and G. Willard [Collins], Bro. Gus [Nichols], Ira North and others really shoveling on the gospel coal we are going to roll on for the Master."[31] Collins, an *Advocate* staff writer, Nashville preacher, and vice president of Lipscomb, and Nichols, an influential north Alabama preacher and *Advocate* staff writer, were among the many church leaders who worked tirelessly to promote the *Advocate*—and thereby Churches of Christ.

Hobbyists

Promoters like North and Collins, and to a degree Nichols, rarely engaged directly in the institutional controversy on the pages of the *Advocate.* Other writers, however, most certainly did, and while they busied themselves writing detailed doctrinal attacks against the *Guardian,* Goodpasture focused on isolating the paper using his editorial page. He portrayed *Guardian* supporters as divisive "hobbyists" and "radical" factionists and suggested that the majority of church members considered their doctrine eccentric. He and many others eventually began referring to these troublemakers as "antis," a derisive term intended to cast them as unreasonable reactionaries in general, not merely anti-institutional.[32] However, as Richard Hughes has observed, although the *Guardian* "shared a common rejection of modernization" with other Church of Christ splinter groups from the past, its doctrinal positions were firmly rooted in the movement's history. In other words, it was misleading to suggest that few church members had ever espoused the viewpoints pushed by the *Guardian.* Nevertheless, Goodpasture skillfully depicted the noninstitutional movement as extreme and regularly questioned the motives of its leading proponents. "Sometimes men arise in the church who have an overweening ambition for first place," he wrote in 1951. "They would rather lead a faction than serve the church." These men "place restrictions where the Lord" did not, and so it was imperative that a stand be taken against "their hurtful extremes and hobbies."[33]

N. B. Hardeman seemed to have an even lower opinion than Goodpasture of the noninstitutional leadership. On one occasion, after labeling *Guardian* editor Yater Tant "a degenerate son of a noble sire," a reference to legendary preacher J. D. Tant, Yater's father, Hardeman described him as "deceptive and dishonest." He was convinced that Goodpasture "must show every honest person how sinful is the Guardian." Indeed, Hardeman and other church leaders considered Goodpasture the leader in the fight against "anti-ism," writing on one occasion, "You must stay well if possible. The Cause needs you as we fight the opposition." Goodpasture likewise saw himself as leading that fight. He obliquely compared his stand against false doctrine in the twentieth century with the apostle Paul's in the first: "Paul stood like a stone wall against the Judaizers. The value of his work in exposing their methods, answering their arguments, and staying their progress is incalculable."[34]

In 1951, in an effort to expose the divisive spirit of the noninstitutional movement, Goodpasture publicized a church dispute in Lufkin, Texas, where Roy Cogdill published the *Guardian.* A bitter division had split the Fourth and Groesbeck congregation in the city. When the dust settled, Cogdill was preaching at the breakaway congregation, while *Guardian* staff writer Cled Wallace was preaching at the established church. The split had nothing to do with the institutional issues, but Goodpasture took advantage of it to ridicule "anti" leaders for their inability to maintain peace among themselves.[35] In his first mention of Lufkin, he raised the question of where editor Tant would worship when visiting the city, with staff writer Wallace or publisher Cogdill? And just what were "the details of 'the Lufkin plan' for *starting* new congregations"? Then, after conferring with N. B. Hardeman, Goodpasture reprinted a guest editorial from a

1933 issue of the *Advocate,* when Foy Wallace was editor. He did not reveal that he, as an *Advocate* staff writer, was the author of that editorial. In an obvious reference to Lufkin, Goodpasture introduced the piece by explaining, "There seems to be a recurring need for just such an article." The editorial upheld the "responsibility" of even a "religious paper to 'mark' and 'avoid' them that cause divisions." Hardeman judged that the editorial would "stop the bragging and the extravagant statements" made by noninstitutional leaders. A month later Goodpasture added insult to injury by publishing a statement from the elders of the established congregation that placed responsibility for the division on Cogdill.[36]

Cogdill and Tant published a stream of articles on "institutionalism" each week, and they were chagrined that Goodpasture had introduced the local church controversy. They believed it was a calculated effort to divert attention from the issues. Their cause suffered serious injury during those months because both Cled and Foy Wallace "dropped out of the fight against institutionalism."[37] Foy Wallace had already abandoned the *Guardian* months earlier and quietly and gradually had begun to align himself with institutional Churches of Christ. The affair at Fourth and Groesbeck pushed Cled in the same direction.[38] Meanwhile, Cogdill and Tant called Goodpasture to task. They criticized him for "meddling" in the Lufkin affair; for his attempts to "disparage, slur, belittle, and otherwise discredit" the *Guardian;* for "carrying a constant flood of articles, advertisements, and news reports that *promote* and *encourage*" institutionalism; and for "refusing a fair discussion of both sides" of the institutional issues. Goodpasture's reply was sharp. He belittled Cogdill, suggesting that he was "the victim of some strange and distracting complex," and he accused Tant and Cogdill of constantly shifting positions: "The publisher and editor of the Guardian study so hard, learn so fast, and change so quickly that it is hard for some of their readers to keep up with them!"[39]

The *Guardian* leadership understood that Goodpasture was using the Lufkin church split to discredit them—as well as the entire noninstitutional movement—and they conveyed this to their readers. "Prodigious efforts are being made to be-cloud the issue," Tant explained, assuring readers that doctrine was at issue, not "personalities." He also took the opportunity to print a "re-statement of convictions," which more or less defined the parameters of the institutional division. Tant stressed that schools and colleges "*are not the work of the church . . . and, hence, cannot be rightfully supported from the church treasury.*" Regarding orphanages, he argued that "the organization of a 'board of benevolence' composed of members of various congregations, acting independently of . . . the local congregation is . . . without authority in God's word." On congregational cooperation in mission work, he asserted that "whenever any 'sponsoring church' seeks in any way at all to exercise oversight over a . . . church in a foreign field, or to relieve other churches . . . of their responsibility in foreign evangelism by spending their money for them, there is a clear violation of New Testament principles." "These are the positions," Tant continued, "that have brought down upon us the wrath . . . of brother Goodpasture." Cogdill charged that Goodpasture had "seized upon the tragic situation at Lufkin as a golden opportunity to discredit *persons*" in an attempt to "destroy the *principles* for which those persons have fought." After defending his role in the Lufkin division and calling into question Goodpasture's character, he assured the *Advocate* editor that his "slimy tactic will not succeed." Even if Goodpasture somehow managed to silence the *Guardian,* "thousands upon multiplied thousands of the Lord's people . . . will stand against the tide of human institutionalism which is sweeping the church."[40]

N. B. Hardeman confided to Goodpasture that Cogdill's response was an "outburst" full of "venom, envy, and jealousy" that "very few will endorse." He advised Goodpasture to resist "the temptation to make [a] full reply," which would only provide fodder for the *Guardian,* suggesting instead "that only a brief statement—or none at all—be made." Goodpasture hewed to Hardeman's strategy, responding only to a single aspect of Cogdill's article. Cogdill had given impetus to a rumor that one of the *Advocate* staff writers had "a standing offer of a $25.00 reward for anyone who visits the Advocate office and hears brother Goodpasture mention any preacher in conversation without trying to knife said preacher in the back before the conversation ends." In refuting the rumor, Goodpasture printed statements from each staff writer denying the charge, and letters from readers who wrote in to claim the reward.[41]

Quarantine

For a time after the Lufkin exchange, the *Advocate* was relatively quiet on the institutional controversy. This was especially true of the editorial page. Goodpasture seemed to be making a concerted effort to keep negatives to a minimum and to give as little attention as possible to the *Guardian.* By 1954, however, his strategy had noticeably changed. He now appeared determined to deal more decisively with the "anti-brethren." In November of that year, he printed a letter from an unnamed church elder suggesting that the *Advocate* "publish a list of the preachers who have been chronic church-busters." The preacher at the elder's congregation had "just left, after stirring up no little trouble." To the membership's dismay, "he turned out to be a rank hairsplitter and hobby rider"—another way of saying he was "anti"—and they "were rather disposed to think that he came with the hidden intention of 'converting the church' to his particular hobbies." The congregation was desperate to avoid another hiring mistake. Goodpasture called this "letter typical of an increasing number coming to our attention." While not endorsing the specific suggestion of publishing a list of troublesome preachers, he was pleased that elders "are more careful . . . to check the records of preachers who may be under consideration for any given work." In an editorial six months earlier, he had recommended that churches exercise care in hiring preachers. He described New Testament Judaizers as being "among the earliest hobby riders to afflict the church" and warned elders to watch out for their "modern successors." Do not be blind to the wiles of preachers who "[seek] to disturb and take over churches," he counseled.[42]

The elder's November letter, and Goodpasture's commendation of it, led directly to a milestone in the institutional controversy. Three weeks after the letter's publication, Goodpasture printed comments from readers who supported the concept of marking noninstitutional preachers. Ira North, for example, surmised that if such a step were taken young preachers would "think twice before devoting their energy and talents to causing confusion and division." Another letter, from an unnamed "faithful brother who has stood like a stone wall against innovations and false doctrines," proved to be especially significant. Goodpasture introduced it with care: "Study carefully what he writes. He is not alone in the treatment he suggests for those who disturb churches with their hobbies." The "faithful brother" suggested that the *Advocate* "might wisely spearhead a movement to 'quarantine' those preachers who today are sowing the seeds of discord among the brotherhood." "The exposure of such men," he reasoned, "may yet prevent many congregations from being disturbed and divided."[43]

Not surprisingly, the *Guardian* howled in response to the suggestion of a preacher "quarantine." Tant and others joined Cogdill in denouncing Goodpasture as a "little man" dangerously "bloated . . . with his own power and importance." For many years, Goodpasture had all but shut the noninstitutional viewpoint out of the *Advocate;* now he was endorsing a plan to shut preachers out of the churches. The growing wedge between the two sides of the institutional debate manifested itself in hyperbole from

Cogdill: "Our brother [Goodpasture] has assumed the attitude of a 'communistic Stalin' and has sought to enclose his 'kingdom' behind an iron curtain. . . . Now he seeks to institute a 'purge' of all who disagree with him and will not 'bow the knee to Baal'—his institutional god." As for Tant, almost three decades later he still expressed anger over Goodpasture's quarantine policy: "Surely Brother Goodpasture's tragic decision [to endorse the quarantine] was one of the most egregious blunders ever made by any editor of a gospel journal in Restoration history!" Tant contended that Goodpasture's approach to doctrinal disagreement held no resemblance to the policies of earlier *Advocate* editors, and thereby caused lines of communication to be broken in a way that inevitably led to division. On the other hand, as David Edwin Harrell has suggested, Goodpasture did what he thought necessary to keep order in Churches of Christ and sustain the group's progress. "From B. C. Goodpasture's point of view," Harrell wrote, "his actions were a reasonable and responsible effort to save the churches from the pillaging of radicals and extremists."[44]

Several months after the recommendation of the quarantine, Goodpasture reported on its progress, and in effect issued another warning: "Elders in particular, and congregations in general, are steering clear of preachers who have the reputation of splitting the churches by their disposition to 'take over' and to 'ventilate' their hobbies." N. B. Hardeman agreed that the quarantine was working and that many were losing patience with the "anti movement." After returning from an extended trip to various parts of Texas, he reported to Goodpasture, "The Guardian crowd doesn't seem to be very popular where I have been." In fact, he judged, the movement had turned "desperate," and he advised Goodpasture not to give the *Guardian* any more free publicity: "If I were editor [Tant's] name would never appear again."[45]

The Confessional

Other evidence that leaders in institutional Churches of Christ had lost patience with the "antis" appeared in 1954 and 1955. Increasing numbers of articles by staff writers and contributors appeared in the *Advocate* challenging noninstitutional views. As prominent *Advocate* staff writer Guy N. Woods put it, the *Advocate*'s "columns [were] opened to us to expose the movement in minute detail." Woods, moreover, was the one who led this charge. Devoting several lengthy articles in 1954 to "Orphanages and Homes for the Aged," Woods addressed a subject now central to the institutional debate. Since the late 1940s, many had argued that Christians should not utilize church-related institutions to care for orphans, widows, and others in need because, according to the New Testament, it was the responsibility of individuals in local congregations to carry out such benevolence. Woods denied that there was only one scriptural way for Christians to care for the needy, and asserted that the orphanages and nursing homes among Churches of Christ were scripturally authorized, organized, and funded. Woods believed that the deluge of articles from him and others created "an informed brotherhood," which once "alerted to [the] aims and methods" of the noninstitutional movement "isolated" it. He may have overstated the case, but the barrage of articles combined with the quarantine produced visible effects, one being the efforts of many preachers to demonstrate clearly which side of the issues they occupied. As Freed-Hardeman College dean E. Claude Gardner observed, preachers accomplished this "through sundry means."[46]

Goodpasture provided one of those "sundry means" beginning in 1957, as he took an additional step to isolate the noninstitutional movement. He began to publish "statements" on the editorial page from preachers who had changed their views on the institutional issues, subtly pressuring others to make similar announcements. The statements indicated that many preachers feared becoming isolated from the mainstream. For a preacher to announce in the *Advocate* that he had changed his views—or that after much study he had finally settled his convictions on the issues—was to ensure that he would not be excluded from the pulpits of mainstream churches, the lectureships of mainstream colleges, and the columns of mainstream papers. Goodpasture had already printed, in 1955, a statement from Foy Wallace disclaiming "any connection at all with the present *Gospel Guardian*," but the first statement in what the *Guardian* would come to call the "confessional" did not appear until 1957. In August of that year, John D. Cox, a preacher in Florence, Alabama, explained to *Advocate* readers that he had arrived at an important conclusion. "It is possible," he declared, "to have congregational cooperation without inter-congregational organization." Goodpasture "congratulated [Cox] on making this clear and forthright statement of his convictions on a vital subject," and he encouraged more of the same from other preachers. "It is heartening," he wrote, "to hear reports from every section of the country concerning able preachers who are making similar announcements. It would be fine if more of these brethren, like our able and highly esteemed Brother Cox, would send us articles and statements." They did. Goodpasture published another twenty statements over the next few years. Especially telling was his introduction to the statement of Charles E. Crouch, a Columbus, Mississippi, preacher. In addition to receiving positive exposure in the *Advocate,* Crouch, apparently out of a job, received an added bonus when announcing the change in his views: a sterling recommendation for employment. Calling Crouch "one of our best young preachers," Goodpasture informed readers that "any congregation needing an able and successful preacher would do well to get in touch with Brother Crouch." Later that year, Crouch began a stint with the Riverwood Church of Christ in Nashville, doubtless providing Roy Cogdill with a perfect example of preachers "willing to sell the truth short and barter away their spiritual birthright for a mere mess of pottage."[47]

Many of the "confessional" statements reflected the fact that controversies over orphanages and the *Herald of Truth,* the nationally syndicated radio and television program funded through a sponsoring-church arrangement, had taken center stage by the late 1950s. Crouch, for example, focused entirely on those two issues as he explained why he had "renounced" his earlier views. "Recent debates, articles which have appeared in the *Gospel Advocate,* and more mature study" had allowed him "to see the inconsistency and error involved in [his] positions." No longer did he believe that "the Herald of Truth type of cooperation" infringed on "congregational autonomy," and, furthermore, he concluded, "the idea that the orphan home is parallel to the Missionary Society is clearly wrong." *Advocate* staff writer Thomas B. Warren reckoned that statements like those from Cox and Crouch were "a manifestation of the fact that the anti movement is losing ground." He expressed gratitude to those who made the statements, and to Goodpasture for publishing them, and "pray[ed] from the heart that every man and woman now connected with the anti movement might also change their minds." The benefit "to the cause of Christ in this and succeeding generations" would be inestimable if they did.[48]

Firm Foundation

An unexpected setback in the *Advocate*'s effort to crush noninstitutionalism came in 1957 when former *Advocate* staff writer Roy H. Lanier, who had only recently resigned, published a series of articles in the *Firm Foundation* seeking middle ground in the orphanage controversy. The *Firm Foundation,* published in Austin, Texas, was another of the oldest and most influential papers among Churches of Christ. Until the publication of Lanier's series, the *Gospel Advocate* and the *Firm Foundation* seemingly were of one mind on the institutional issues. Lanier revealed that further study had convinced him that a church-related orphan home was scripturally organized only if it was under the oversight of a single eldership, not a board; otherwise it was parallel to a missionary society—an entity larger than the local church carrying out the work of the church. Reuel Lemmons, editor of the *Firm Foundation* since 1955, expressed agreement with Lanier, increasing the sense of crisis for the *Advocate.* Guy Woods responded forcefully—and from the *Advocate*'s editorial page—once again denying that orphanages and other benevolent institutions among Churches of Christ had any parallel whatsoever to missionary societies. He also made something of a threat to Lanier and Lemmons: "We are sorry that Brother Lanier has seen fit to raise this issue at this juncture. We believe his articles will result in harm to himself, to the journal in which it appeared, and to the cause of Christ."[49]

This dangerous rift in the ranks of those trying to quarantine the "anti-brethren" persisted. A year later, in 1958, Lemmons wrote an editorial restating Lanier's arguments. On the *Advocate*'s editorial page, Woods called the piece "shocking." "Radicals and extremists among us," he lamented, "will gleefully hail it as evidence of divided sentiment among those who have hitherto presented a solid phalanx against those troublers in Israel." N. B. Hardeman surmised that "Bro. Guy has certainly fixed Bro. Lemmons," but it was another year before Goodpasture was able to announce that the two influential papers had closed ranks. In March 1959 he published a statement signed by several men, himself included, revealing that in January at the Freed-Hardeman College lectureship Lemmons had expressed a view on the orphan home issue in line with the views of institutional leaders. One of the signatories, Freed-Hardeman president H. A. Dixon, explained that Lemmons had "stated that in his judgment it was better to establish [orphan] homes under the oversight of elders, but that he did not make this the law governing such endeavors." Dixon was pleased that Lemmons held "the view that the organization of these homes, and their support by churches lie in the realm of human judgment," and he knew that others would likewise "rejoice" and "join [him] in sending new and renewal subscriptions" to Lemmons in honor of the *Firm Foundation*'s seventy-fifth anniversary. Dixon was not putting words in Lemmons's mouth. In a letter to Goodpasture shortly after the Freed-Hardeman lectureship, Lemmons confirmed that he had indeed closed ranks with the *Advocate* and other institutional leaders. He encouraged Goodpasture to be present at the upcoming Abilene Christian College lectureship in order to help celebrate the *Firm Foundation*'s anniversary.

"I think it would mean a great deal," he wrote, "to demonstrate the solidarity and unity we mention if we could present about the same group at the Firm Foundation luncheon [as] presented a few years ago at the Gospel Advocate dinner during the Lectures."[50]

Florida Christian College

From the early 1950s, Goodpasture had demonstrated a willingness to write off the most zealous and cantankerous of the "antis," especially the leaders of the *Gospel Guardian.* By the end of the decade, during the breach with the *Firm Foundation,* he was also ready to be done with some of the movement's more moderate leaders, including the administration and faculty of Florida Christian College (FCC) in Tampa. In his dealings with FCC at this point, as with his earlier encounters with controversy, Goodpasture made skillful use of "the efficiency of [the] informal political structures" of Churches of Christ.[51] Although FCC had leaned toward noninstitutional positions since the late 1940s, its leadership, particularly President James R. Cope and Bible department head Homer Hailey, had "sustained a strained relationship" with the *Advocate.* By the late 1950s, that relationship had become virtually nonexistent.[52]

The *Advocate*'s final break from FCC began with the defection of one of its Bible faculty members, Pat Hardeman, nephew of N. B. Hardeman. In March 1958 he published a statement in the *Advocate* "confessional" column calling on his "former colleagues" to follow his example and "abandon their extreme views." Over the next several months, Hardeman wrote more articles criticizing FCC and the *Guardian.*[53] His uncle predicted that those writings would "cause Tant and Cope no little trouble," and that "it may turn out that it was good for him to have been one of them and now knows whereof he speaks." Then Pat Hardeman unexpectedly became a liability to Goodpasture when he left Churches of Christ altogether, affiliating with the liberal Unitarian Fellowship of Tampa. Goodpasture had no choice but to distance the *Advocate* from Hardeman, but not before suggesting that the severe treatment he received from "his erstwhile companions in hobbyism" may have pushed him to his "present condition."[54]

Nevertheless, with Hardeman's articles against FCC, the isolation of the college had begun. In July 1958, Goodpasture caused a stir when he published a full-page advertisement for FCC.[55] The ad did not mention the institutional issues, but many loyal readers were shocked and disappointed that Goodpasture let it appear, and wrote to tell him so. Goodpasture provided "a glimpse of the letters" by publishing ten. One correspondent wrote, "Personally, I would not use my influence to urge a young man or woman to attend Florida Christian College." Another remarked that FCC "has become among our colleges what the *Gospel Guardian* has among the papers." Yet another related a conversation with a church elder in north Alabama who "told [him] with grief and a broken heart that Florida Christian College had made an 'anti' out of his boy." Goodpasture acknowledged that he had been unsure about running the ad, but explained, "As long as there is reasonable hope of rescuing a college from its unsound teaching, it has been our policy to carry its advertisements." He expressed "hope that enough of the board members [would] wake up to what is happening in time to save the college," but at the same time made it clear that he agreed with the letter writers. Church members would be wise to avoid FCC, he warned: "Congregations again and again, when seeking a preacher, have told me that they would not consider a preacher who had attended FCC." The attack on FCC had the intended effect. Eddie G. Couch, minister of the prestigious San Jose Church of Christ in Jacksonville, Florida, offered to help Goodpasture apply political pressure against FCC. He asked for one hundred copies of the issue so that he could distribute it to church leaders in Jacksonville, a city with "at least two churches . . . served by preachers from Florida Christian College who hold to anti-cooperation views."[56] More skirmishing was to come, but the isolation of FCC signaled that the institutional division was practically complete.

To Speak the Same Thing

Looking back in 1959 on his twenty years as editor of the *Gospel Advocate,* B. C. Goodpasture made what many would have regarded a disingenuous statement: "Frequently I have said that I was the only person in the brotherhood who did not know how to run it!" In fact, for a number of years Goodpasture—insofar as any one person could exercise such power in such a diffuse movement—had rather effectively been "running" Churches of Christ as a quintessential "editor-bishop." In 1955 two *Advocate* contributors accurately described the informal but highly influential role of the editor and his paper. According to John E. Kirk, since Churches of Christ "have no conventions or convocations," papers like the *Advocate* serve the "brotherhood" by "acting as a clearinghouse for news regarding the growth, location, and activities of the church in the various parts of the world." This "function" was in addition to a paper's role in "spreading, defending and vindicating the gospel" and "warn[ing] brethren of impending dangers." James D. Groves similarly pointed out that "a paper like the *Advocate* keeps Christians in touch with kindred activities," while delivering "the unceasing truth." Moreover, he asserted, quoting I Corinthians 1:10, "a good, true, gospel paper will help the church to 'speak the same thing.' There is no apostle, no Jerusalem church to guide with wisdom, only the word to speak with authority, hence the clear word of God must be explained, must be made clear by the finest minds willing to write. It must be trumpeted abroad and the preaching of far-flung messengers measured by the word. A paper helps to keep order and unity." Churches of Christ have been described as a "wild democracy" that built cohesiveness and delineated division by the same means: through the formation of institutional networks.[57] At the head of this democracy's most influential institution, B. C. Goodpasture joined with like-minded institutions and leaders to impose a semblance of order, while also doing much to define the character of postwar Churches of Christ.

7
Northern Millenarian Fundamentalism in the South, 1900–1950

B. Dwain Waldrep

Scholars of religion in the South have often argued for its distinctive character, a trait rooted in the region's unique history and accompanying social and cultural isolationism. A shared history and isolationism combined to produce a remarkable uniformity in religious beliefs and practices throughout the South. This traditional narrative of southern religious life was, in part, shaped by an emphasis upon studies of mainstream Protestants in the South and upon what separated them from their northern counterparts. As essays in this work demonstrate, David Edwin Harrell Jr. and others have done much in recent decades to remedy the unbalanced historiography of the region's religious life by studying forms of belief and practice outside the South's Protestant mainstream and by reexamining the history of the mainstream denominations with an eye to divergent trends. This study addresses another neglected aspect of southern evangelicalism's history, the forging of significant ties with elements within northern evangelicalism and the shaping influence these ties exerted upon the history of fundamentalism in the South, which led to the development of a variant form of evangelicalism in the region.

These developments began in the decades after 1900, when itinerant, millenarian Bible teachers extended the northern prophetic and Bible conference movement into the urban South, where they largely attracted mainstream Protestants, particularly Southern Baptists and Southern Presbyterians. This movement, which arose during the late nineteenth century, was distinguished by its advocacy of dispensational premillennialism.[1] The success enjoyed by these northern Bible teachers was a product of widespread southern evangelical interest in dispensationalism, and it enabled them to generate a substantial branch of the millenarian fundamentalist movement in the South. Due to the region's social and cultural conservatism and to its aversion to northern influences, the southern wing of the millenarian fundamentalist movement was not simply a mirror image of its northern counterpart. Its adherents selectively absorbed elements of northern fundamentalism that correlated with the South's more conservative environment and rejected the movement's more negative features associated with its opposition to liberal developments in the North.[2]

These Bible teachers were often associated with Dwight L. Moody's revivalist empire and were typically invited into the region by southern evangelicals who had profited from Moody's ministry. Baptist pastor Leonard G. Broughton, for example, attended Moody's Northfield Bible conferences in the 1890s and, with Moody's encouragement, launched an annual Bible conference schedule in 1889 at the Tabernacle Baptist Church in Atlanta, Georgia. Broughton's conferences drew thousands of southern evangelicals and regularly featured speakers from Northfield and from Moody Bible Institute (MBI) in Chicago.[3] Nor were the South's small towns unaffected by northern fundamentalism's reach. At the advice of Baptist evangelist Mordecai F. Ham, John Christopher Cowell Jr. of Fayetteville, North Carolina, attended MBI in the 1920s and subsequently became a full-time Baptist evangelist. In 1934 he accepted a pastoral call from Central Baptist Church in Decatur, Alabama, where he launched a regular program of Bible conferences featuring such northern fundamentalist speakers as C. I. Scofield, Harry Ironside, Arno C. Gaebelein, William Bell Riley, and William L. Pettingill. Cowell often traveled to Chicago to speak at MBI and hired Moody graduates as staff members at Central Baptist. Not surprisingly, scores of young people from Central Baptist enrolled at MBI. They absorbed its fundamentalist theology and returned to the South, where they helped broaden MBI's influence in the region. In 1938 alone, MBI staff conducted 694 Bible conferences in the South, drawing countless southern evangelicals into northern fundamentalism's orbit.[4]

As important as MBI was to developing southern interest in dispensational premillennialism, by midcentury the Dallas Theological Seminary (DTS) surpassed its influence. Historians of American fundamentalism have consistently recognized DTS as the "academic and ideological Vatican" of dispensationalism in America.[5] DTS was founded in 1924 by C. I. Scofield's protégé, Lewis Sperry Chafer, who began conducting Bible conferences in the South in 1903.[6] Because of liberal denominational developments, Chafer saw Bible conferences, especially those promoting dispensationalism, as an important conservative force within American Christianity. By the 1920s he believed that this "wide-spread and increasingly effective Bible movement" was threatened by the declining strength of its aging first generation leaders. He was convinced that neither the liberal denominational divinity schools nor the conservative northern Bible institutes would produce well-trained dispensational ministers to continue the work of these aging Bible conference teachers. The Bible conference movement, he observed, "is peculiarly a work of God," and "no general organization has been called into being to foster or direct the work." In founding DTS, Chafer institutionalized the Bible conference movement and ensured its survival by training expositors to continue the movement's ministry.[7]

Although DTS was located in the South, it was not southern in origin. Chafer and his principal advisors in founding the seminary were prominent evangelicals who had participated in the northern Bible conference movement of the late nineteenth and early twentieth centuries. Chafer was a Presbyterian evangelist and Bible teacher, with a northern Congregational background. Alexander B. Winchester, who served as visiting faculty in English Bible, was a Canadian Presbyterian pastor and Bible conference speaker. William Henry Griffith-Thomas was a theologian of international repute and a leader within the evangelical wing of the Church of England, who had retired in 1919 from Wycliffe College, Toronto, Canada, to pursue Bible conference ministry.[8] Thus DTS had a distinctly northern flavor, and the institution exhibited Chafer's soft or nonconfrontational form of fundamentalism, which he learned from his mentor, C. I. Scofield. Scofield advised Chafer not to engage in "controversy" but to "give out the positive word" of God's truth. Chafer lamented the rancorous fundamentalist rhetoric used by William Bell Riley and J. Frank Norris, who were in the forefront of American fundamentalism. Chafer expressed a lack of sympathy with the movement, "largely," he explained, because "it has been negative in its testimony."[9] In the decades after its founding, DTS gave birth to a loosely affiliated network of independent parachurch institutions and nondenominational churches in the South that were marked by a similar moderate position on the defense of Christian truth.

Chafer's success in forming a southern wing of the northern millenarian movement in the South can, in part, be accounted for by the foundation he built through the Bible conference movement. Beyond that available foundation, his success can further be explained by two central fundamentalist traits associated with the Bible conference speakers. First, their expository teaching style proved highly attractive to southerners who had grown tired of a steady diet of evangelistic and moralistic sermons in their churches, a preaching style that prevailed in the South after the "Great Revival" of the early nineteenth century.[10] Second, the rise of theological liberalism in the North, World War I, and the Great Depression seemed to validate the dispensational depiction of the end times. Like thousands of their northern counterparts, many southern evangelicals believed that dispensationalism made sense of the Scriptures and eagerly sought opportunities to learn from dispensational Bible teachers.

Beyond Chafer's personal influence and that of DTS was the influence of approximately twelve independent, dispensational Bible schools loosely affiliated with DTS. These institutions were founded in several of the South's larger cities between 1928 and 1950 with manpower and inspiration provided by MBI and DTS. Seven of these schools remain in operation: Southern Bible Institute (formerly Dallas Colored Bible Institute) in Dallas, Texas, founded in 1928 by Edmund Ironside, Harry Ironside's eldest son; Baltimore School of the Bible (formerly the School of Biblical Research, then the Fellowship of Bible Study) in Baltimore, Maryland, founded in 1931 by Baptists and Presbyterians influenced by A. C. Dixon, a distinguished Southern Baptist pastor with intimate ties to D. L. Moody; Southeastern Bible College (formerly Birmingham School of the Bible) in Birmingham, Alabama, founded in 1933 by Edgar J. Rowe, a Southern Baptist layman; Chattanooga Bible Institute, founded in 1933 in Chattanooga, Tennessee, by H. E. Wright, assistant to T. Berry Brannon on the Radio Revival broadcast and a staff member at Chattanooga's First Presbyterian Church; Carver Bible College (formerly Carver Bible Institute) in Atlanta, Georgia, founded by MBI alumni Talmage and Grace Payne; Crichton College (formerly Mid-South Bible Institute), founded in 1941 by DTS alumnus Thomas McKinney; and Appalachian Bible College (formerly Appalachian Bible Institute) in Bradley, West Virginia, founded in 1950 by MBI alumnus Lester Pipkin. Dispensationalism's increasing popularity among southern evangelicals, particularly among rank-and-file Presbyterians and Baptists, can be attributed to laypersons attending Bible conferences and, more importantly, to their enrollment in these nondenominational Bible schools. Large numbers of Chafer's graduates served as administrators and taught in these institutes. The Bible schools' importance as purveyors of dispensationalism can hardly be overstated.

Due to regional patterns of development, nondenominational Bible institutes in the South initially shared only a few of northern fundamentalism's early twentieth-century interests. Specifically, they were modeled on MBI's educational structure and promoted the Bible conference movement's teaching style, premillennialism, and Keswick spirituality. Alongside these northern-derived traits, the schools also reflected southern evangelicalism's ethos and primary concerns, particularly its emphasis on evangelism and moral rectitude.

The differences between northern and southern Bible institutes in the 1930s and 1940s arose from the contrasting social and cultural environments of the two regions. As the Bible school movement spread across the South, fundamentalists in the North were embracing an "alienated 'faithful remnant' stance" toward their culture. As historian Joel Carpenter observed, northern fundamentalists entered the 1930s in turmoil and bore the "social and psychic burden" often endured by outsiders.[11] By the end of the Great Depression, Christian Smith noted that fundamentalism "had evolved into a somewhat reclusive and defensive version of its nineteenth-century self."[12]

Southern evangelicals, on the other hand, did not share—at least in the same sense—the denominational turmoil, cultural isolation, and sense of alienation that afflicted northern fundamentalists. Nondenominational Bible schools in the South were strongly tied to middle-class Baptists and Presbyterians in the New South's larger cities. These mainline southern evangelicals were just beginning to face some of the modernist influences faced previously by northern evangelicals. "In the South," George Marsden noted, "evangelicalism was still a virtually unchallenged establishment."[13] Even progressive political and social movements, observed historian George Tindall, tended to be marked in the South by traditionalism, individualism, and a "unique moral-religious tone" derived from the "fundamental conditioning influence of the churches."[14] On the whole, widely divergent social and cultural differences confronted northern and southern evangelicals in the early twentieth century, and they generally displayed opposing religious attitudes. Consequently, southern evangelicals were little affected by northern fundamentalism's siege mentality when they founded southern Bible institutes.

Thus southern Bible institutes sustained a sense of mission and character essentially different from their contemporary northern counterparts. In an economic environment marked by inadequate resources for the "competent training of laymen," southern Bible schools filled an acutely felt need for access to quality religious education.[15] Like Bible schools in the North, southern schools began as evening institutes for training laypersons and evolved into day schools dedicated to providing vocational training for young people desiring to enter full-time Christian service. Leaders in southern Bible schools consciously modeled their institutions on MBI's operations and sometimes publicly advertised their links to MBI, drawing on its prestige and relating their ministry to its well-known founder. For example, when soliciting opinions on the need for a day-school program to augment the night classes of Mid-South Bible Institute in Memphis, Tennessee, its founder and president, DTS graduate Thomas McKinney, informed area pastors that Mid-South wanted to provide a "complete Bible Institute program patterned after the work offered by the Moody Bible Institute of Chicago."[16] Southern schools initially borrowed their curriculum structure from MBI's early course of study, which was organized into five sections: Bible Introduction, which covered the Bible's inspiration as well as the structure and methods of Bible study; Bible Doctrine, consisting of courses in systematic theology; Study of the Bible, comprised of expository lectures that surveyed Bible books; Analysis, in which students utilized study methods on selected Scripture passages and constructed and delivered presentations based on their work; and Methods of Work, which covered personal evangelism and familiarized students with approaches to city, home, and foreign mission work.[17]

While southern Bible schools shared a nationally exhibited curricular structure modeled after MBI's curriculum, it was DTS that set their practical agenda, teaching conservative theology within a dispensationalist framework to enable laypersons to fulfill their responsibilities in spreading the gospel through Sunday school and missions work. Chafer believed that Bible institutes played a crucial role in lay education. "Too much effort cannot be made," he emphasized, "to develop every Sunday School teacher and every mission worker to the fullest degree and to increase the number by every means." The highest trained men are to teach students "pursuing advanced courses, while these, in turn, direct, train, and stimulate the great army who carry on the layman's testimony."[18] Like many fundamentalists then and now, Chafer also emphasized the necessity of grounding laypersons in "sound doctrine." The believer lacking such instruction, he warned, would be easy prey for false teachers and false systems of belief.[19] The widespread use of literature published by professors at DTS and the prominence of Chafer's alumni on their faculties essentially made southern Bible institutes extension centers of the seminary. As these schools emerged across the region, they, along with cooperating mainline churches, became the principal sponsors of Bible conferences in the South. These schools significantly extended and reinforced DTS's influence within the Southern Presbyterian and Southern Baptist denominations, particularly among their rank-and-file members.

As DTS's influence among Southern Presbyterians and Southern Baptists grew, many of those denomination's leaders began to criticize the seminary and the Bible schools. By 1940 their opposition intensified, as Presbyterian and Baptist leaders felt they had sufficient evidence to view northern-influenced nondenominational fundamentalism as a corrosive movement that weakened denominational loyalty among southern evangelicals.

Mainline denominational opposition to northern influence should be viewed within the broader context of enduring sectional distrust between the North and the South. Some southern denominational leaders distrusted northern fundamentalism as much as they did modernism, identifying both as northern products that promoted "union under a new set of values or doctrines."[20] For most of the nineteenth century, southern denominations had been agents of southern nationalism, upholding fidelity to regional ways of life, a long tradition of sectional feeling, and self-imposed isolation. In an 1871 Confederate Memorial Day address in Charleston, South Carolina, Presbyterian minister John L. Girardeau expressed sectionalist sentiments that resonated among southern evangelicals well into the twentieth century. Girardeau warned his fellow southerners that postwar conditions left them exposed to the "invasion of theories and the pressures of influences which were excluded by the settled conditions of the past." This threat already existed in the sphere of religion, he stated, so "it becomes us to watch against tendencies which carry in them the seeds of defection from a pure religious faith." This could be accomplished, he informed his listeners, by clinging to "our identity as a people," by "instamping on the minds of our children principles hallowed by the blood of patriots."[21] Southern evangelicals, even those participating in the northern Bible conference movement, evidently followed this advice. At the beginning of the twentieth century, historian Samuel Hill wrote, southern culture remained sectionalist "by choice, by dint of memory, and by virtue of public circumstances."[22] In religion, historian Wayne Flynt observed, sectionalist sentiments meant that few southern evangelicals surmounted "religious localism on behalf of any transcending theology, whether liberal or fundamentalist. They were religious in their own way, according to the values and assumptions of their region."[23]

During the 1940s, when opposition to DTS's influence intensified, southern evangelicals were facing the decline of southern geographical and cultural isolation and were struggling with increasing religious and social changes wrought by outside forces. Viewed from this perspective, southern evangelical leaders saw DTS and its associated Bible schools as another alien force threatening traditional beliefs and southern denominational integrity. Within the Southern Presbyterian Church (PCUS), which was undergoing strife over proposals to reunite with the Northern Presbyterian Church (PCUSA), denominational leaders opposed DTS on theological grounds and sought to purge dispensationalists from their ranks by arguing that dispensationalism violated the church's doctrinal standards. Southern Baptist traditionalists, on the other hand, lacked denominational authority and an ecclesiastical court system that would have enabled them to remove DTS's influence from convention churches, so they took the opposite approach. Traditionalists within the Southern Baptist Convention (SBC) sought to keep their constituency away from DTS and the independent Bible schools by warning them of the dangers involved and by providing educational alternatives to the Bible institutes.

James E. Bear, professor of New Testament at Union Theological Seminary in Virginia, initiated the theological confrontation between DTS and PCUS officials. In July 1938, Bear published an article in the *Union Seminary Review* in which he argued that Scofield and Chafer's dispensational premillennialism conflicted with the Westminster Confession of Faith.[24] That same year, the East Mississippi Presbytery petitioned the General Assembly to halt the dissemination of dispensationalism with the church. Although the assembly declined to act, it was evident that a showdown between DTS and PCUS leaders was in the offing.[25] Social liberals within the PCUS also promoted opposition to dispensationalism, hoping to create a rift within conservative forces and draw attention away from the controversy surrounding their efforts to reunite the PCUS with the PCUSA.[26] Albert Sidney Johnson, pastor of the First Presbyterian Church in Charlotte, North Carolina, warned Chafer that liberals were using dispensationalism to create such a rift and advised him to tread carefully so as not to damage conservative efforts against the "destructive Modernism and infidelity" that would be brought into the PCUS by liberals within the PCUSA.[27]

In April 1940, the North Alabama Presbytery brought the conflict to a head by petitioning the PCUS General Assembly to clarify the denomination's view toward dispensationalism. Presbytery officials sought the General Assembly's advice concerning proper credentials for a candidate seeking ordination, with particular questions about candidates from institutions advocating dispensationalism. It also asked for a clear statement concerning the church's attitude toward both applicants and current ministers espousing dispensationalism. Although it had declined to act in 1938, the General Assembly responded to mounting concerns about dispensationalism in 1940 by placing the overture on the agenda for the next annual meeting.[28]

The 1941 General Assembly assigned the overture to the Ad Interim Committee on Changes in Confession of Faith and Catechisms, which spent the next several years examining whether or not dispensationalism and PCUS's confession of faith were compatible.[29] DTS's relationship to the PCUS became clear in 1943, when the committee of the General Assembly issued a preliminary statement, which, Chafer hyperbolically wrote, cited him as "the chief heretic."[30] Indeed, the report copiously quoted Chafer's 1936 article defending dispensationalism and identified him as its major advocate within the denomination. The committee noted that dispensationalism had influenced many congregations within the church, producing disloyalty to PCUS agencies. Many of these congregations, the report asserted, habitually used interdenominational Sunday school materials, disparaged denominational agencies, and diverted funds to "so-called 'Faith Missions' and 'Interdenominational Bible Institutes.'"[31] After writing six pages detailing the theological differences between dispensationalism and traditional beliefs, the committee concluded by citing its disagreement with Chafer's dispensational theology. "Dispensationalism and the teaching of the Confession," they concluded, "belong to two different systems of Bible interpretation."[32] In its final report, which was adopted at the General Assembly meeting in 1944, the committee effectively ended DTS's influence within the PCUS by asserting that dispensationalism was diametrically and indisputably opposed to the "system of doctrine set forth in the Confession of Faith."[33] Chafer's alumni maintained a small presence within the PCUS after 1945, but his ambition for the seminary to serve Southern Presbyterians had been effectively derailed. Thereafter, some Presbyterians within DTS's PCUS constituency separated from their churches and entered the ranks of the developing independent Bible church movement being forged by DTS faculty members and Chafer's alumni within the Bible schools.

Circumstances differed somewhat within the Southern Baptist Convention, yet its opposition to DTS and the Bible institutes sprang from a similar desire to exclude northern influences that threatened denominational purity. Leaders within the SBC sought to remove DTS's influence upon their denomination because it represented a form of northern ecumenism that injured denominational loyalty and weakened adherence to Baptist theological distinctives.

Southern Baptist leaders were concerned about DTS and the Bible schools because interdenominational schools emphasized only a few essential doctrines and promoted cooperation with independent faith agencies for fulfilling the Great Commission. Baptists traditionally gave priority to the independence of local congregations as contrasted to wider forms of cooperative work, insisted upon Baptist-administered immersions, and restricted representation in the convention to its local churches. Although Southern Baptists had explored ecumenical forms of fellowship and ministry between 1880 and World War I, James B. Gambrell's 1919 presidential address emphasized denominational efficiency and forged a consensus against ecumenical alliances. For much of the twentieth century, Southern Baptists generally espoused a policy of "skeptical noninvolvement" in liberal or conservative ecumenical partnerships.[34]

During the 1920s, most Southern Baptists refused to forge ecumenical alliances with fundamentalist organizations such as the World's Christian Fundamentals Association (WCFA). Lee R. Scarborough, president of Southwestern Theological Seminary, expressed a consensus view when he called the WCFA an "unbridled horse" and asserted that he could not join any interdenominational organization that proposed to "teach fundamentals to Baptist churches."[35] This consensus against ecumenical alliances forged by Gambrell and reinforced by leaders such as Scarborough formed the historical context of Southern Baptist reaction to DTS and the nondenominational Bible schools.

In particular, Baptist concerns flowed from fear of the overemphasis on the universal nature of the body of Christ at DTS and in the Bible schools. Baptist editor O. W. Taylor noted that Baptist preachers who had studied at such schools often led churches away from denominational loyalty by teaching the "universal invisible church theory, open communion, alien immersion and so on."[36]

In response to this threat, pastors and convention leaders embarked on a passionate critique of interdenominational schools and sought ways to prevent Southern Baptists from attending these institutions. Taylor, denominational leader and editor of the *Baptist and Reflector*, led the way by criticizing the tendency of interdenominational schools to emphasize indispensable versus nonessential doctrines. Such schools may be orthodox on redemptive fundamentals such as the death, burial, and resurrection of Christ, he wrote, but God also demanded obedience in such things as Baptism, the Lord's Supper, and missions. Taylor believed that the nonsectarian nature of interdenominational teaching necessarily implied disloyalty to the Bible, a charge repeated by many Baptist pastors and denominational officials.[37]

In an article titled "Northern Fundamentalism," Duke McCall, president of Southern Baptist Theological Seminary, warned Southern Baptists to beware of "right-wing interdenominationalists" who "always major on one or two doctrines which are widely held among Christians but ignore the Bible at other points such as baptism."[38] Another Baptist writer, R. Lofton Hudson of Chattanooga, Tennessee, concurred and censured interdenominational schools for elevating premillennialism as a fundamental article of faith while placing "little importance on such matters as water baptism and the Lord's Supper. . . . When did the truth about Christ's visible return become necessary to the saving of a soul?" he asked.[39] Like other Baptist leaders, Hudson believed that interdenominational teaching minimized some doctrines for the sake of unity and, thus, was not loyal to the entire Word of God. Fundamentalism, he charged, "is a new kind of modernism" that "invites nondescript interdenominationalists into Baptist pulpits, where hitherto 'the whole counsel of God' has been declared." In drawing Baptists into their schools, Hudson argued, interdenominational teachers dishonestly steal "some of the fruit of Southern Baptist labours."[40]

During the 1940s and 1950s, many Baptist leaders issued calls for denominational integrity and for the proper indoctrination of Baptist young people. Russell Bradley Jones agreed with the editor of the *Word and Way*, who conservatively estimated that 2,500 or more Baptist young people were studying for the ministry in interdenominational schools. He warned denominational leaders that these students "may some day seek to lead Southern Baptists into church unionism," and he called for increased emphasis on the importance of denominational schools and seminaries.[41] "No denomination can long thrive," Norris Gilliam reminded Southern Baptists, without training its own leadership, Baptists must be trained "from the viewpoint of Baptist faith and polity."[42] According to an editorial in the *Baptist and Reflector*, W. Barry Garrett, editor of the *Arizona Baptist Beacon*, surveyed sixty-five Baptist leaders in October 1951 about the threat posed by interdenominational institutions. Their responses revealed widespread concern about the potential loss of denominational distinctiveness.[43]

Baptist leaders continued to criticize interdenominational fundamentalist agencies throughout the 1950s, and they also began to explore positive means to prevent their flocks from affiliating with such institutions. Baptist pastors across the South sought to educate their churches to the dangers of the interdenominational movement. In an article in the *Arkansas Baptist,* W. Ross Edwards reiterated oft-repeated arguments against interdenominationalism and recommended a practical program to strengthen denominational loyalty. He appealed to pastors to educate their churches about the denomination's cooperative program and schools and to emphasize the importance of supporting denominational enterprises. At the same time he implored pastors to urge Baptists not to financially support independent schools and causes, to discourage young people from attending non-Baptist schools, and to caution young Baptist preachers that attendance at such a school would disqualify them from receiving assistance from Baptist leaders in obtaining a Baptist church pastorate. Noting that circumstances required directness, Edwards dramatically resolved "to speak and to write and to do all that I can to warn our people in time, so help me God!"[44]

T. C. Gardner, director of the Baptist Training Union of Texas, wrote a similar warning about the rapidly growing interdenominational youth organizations. He specifically identified Miracle Book Club, Youth for Christ, and Young Life Club as threats to denominational youth ministries for Baptist young people. Youth affiliating with these groups, he warned, might become disillusioned with the denomination, be challenged to financially support nondenominational youth work, and be encouraged to attend nondenominational colleges. He encouraged Baptist associational leaders to fight such influences by intensifying local Baptist youth ministry programs.[45]

Convention leaders and pastors in Baptist churches throughout the South joined Jones, Gilliam, Garrett, and Edwards in their alarm at interdenominationalism's growing strength in the region. In 1953, Gardner, who chaired the Southern Baptist Convention's Committee on Relations with Other Religious Bodies, surveyed association moderators, convention officials, and pastors in every state to determine the efforts being made to inform Baptists about the ordinances, message, mission, program, and commission of the local church. The committee issued a report at the convention meeting in Houston, Texas, in May 1953, highlighting the growing threat posed by interdenominational schools, youth, and mission organizations. "Southern Baptists," the report stated, "are confronted today as never before in their history with the problems growing out of interdenominationalism and non-denominationalism."[46] The report reminded Southern Baptists that the convention organization was based on the "conviction that local, visible, sovereign New Testament churches are the only divine and authorative [*sic*] institutions for carrying out the Great Commission."[47]

Gardner's 1953 report included a litany of what local churches should be doing to resist the influence of interdenominational organizations. Baptists must refuse to ordain anyone not fully subscribing to Baptist doctrines and practices. Pastors should do more expository and doctrinal preaching and lead their churches in observing a "Baptist doctrine week" annually. All new church members should be required to attend a class on Baptist doctrines, and all members should be enlisted in Training Union and Sunday school. Church organizations should be staffed with doctrinally orthodox men and women, who modeled "New Testament principles and ideals."[48] Finally, Southern Baptist officials should include more doctrine lessons in Sunday school and Training Union quarterlies. To make sure the report received widespread attention, Gardner mailed a copy to all of the Baptist newspapers, along with the admonition that Southern Baptists "should ever be on the alert to safeguard our doctrinal purity and denominational integrity."[49] In July, Gardner reported to Porter Routh, executive secretary of the Southern Baptist Convention, that pastors and denominational leaders all over the country were responding favorably to the committee's report.[50]

In addition to ongoing criticism of interdenominational schools and the positive recommendations for responding at the local church level to such institutions, Southern Baptists also discussed ways to provide Baptist educational alternatives to interdenominational Bible institutes. At its 1949 annual meeting, the convention's Theological Survey Committee recommended that Baptist colleges and seminaries study the successful extension program at Howard College in Birmingham, Alabama, and utilize it to form an extension service for their institutions. Howard's program began in 1946, the same year that Southeastern Bible School launched its first extension site in Montgomery, Alabama. Gilbert L. Guffin, who directed Howard's new extension program, established extension centers throughout Alabama to provide biblical instruction and practical training for church workers and preachers who were unable to attend college or seminary. The college staffed these centers with local Baptist pastors and awarded certificates for lay workers and preachers who completed the required courses. In part, Howard's plan was attractive to convention officials because its extension agenda paralleled the educational program of interdenominational Bible schools.[51]

In addition to recommending Howard's program, the committee also suggested the appointment of a new committee to study the work of Bible schools and to ascertain whether or not the convention should establish its own Bible institute to "serve the host of God-called preachers" unable to attend colleges or seminaries.[52] Some Baptists, particularly the handful of Baptists who had already founded their own schools, wanted the convention to operate its own Bible institute.[53] Others rejected the idea of establishing institutes. For instance, in a 1949 article in the *Baptist and Reflector*, George C. Humphrey of Baylor University wrote that instead of establishing institutes, which typically lacked quality liberal arts courses, Baptist universities and colleges should establish strong Bible departments and provide ministerial training for preachers. Capable young preachers without high school diplomas, he argued, could enter such a program after passing proficiency examinations demonstrating an ability to do college work. Responding to fresh, if contrary, ideas in 1950, the committee recommended against the convention operating its own Bible schools. Additionally, the committee recommended that the Inter-Seminary Council expand the extension work being done by convention-sponsored seminaries.[54]

Leaders within the three Baptist Bible institutes begun in the 1940s continued to press for convention-sponsored Bible schools. As a result, the convention's executive committee recommended in 1953 that a special committee be appointed to make a thorough analysis of the need for Bible schools. F. Russell Purdy, a member of the newly formed committee, corresponded with every state secretary, asking each to evaluate the influence of interdenominational Bible institutes in their states and to assess whether or not the convention should sponsor its own institutes. Almost all the respondents argued that Southern Baptists needed denominationally sponsored institutes to meet the needs of the large number of Baptists already attending interdenominational schools. The few who doubted the wisdom of entering this field of education believed that Southern Baptist seminaries could make accommodations to meet the needs of people attending interdenominational Bible institutes. All of Purdy's respondents provided criticisms of the interdenominational Bible school movement, identifying it as a grave problem for Southern Baptists.[55]

Despite strong lobbying from the presidents of the handful of existing

Baptist Bible institutes, the committee's report once again recommended against convention-supported Bible schools. The committee noted the growing success of the Seminary Extension Department, a cooperative project of the Southern Baptist seminaries established in 1951, and argued that this effort coupled with the extension center programs operated by many Baptist colleges sufficiently met the threat posed by interdenominationalism.[56]

Despite tenacious efforts, Southern Baptists were less successful than the PCUS in their efforts to curtail Dallas Seminary's influence. First, Baptists simply lacked the ecclesiastical authority to dictate to local churches. Second, Baptist broadmindedness on millennial interpretations left the door open for greater interdenominational influence. And third, DTS and the Bible institutes provided dispensational premillennial teaching generally unavailable from Baptist sources. Not until 1984, when the trustees of the Baptist Sunday School Board issued guidelines ensuring that forms of premillennialism be included alongside amillennialism in church literature and convention press publications, did the Southern Baptist Convention approve of the teaching.[57] In the years after 1960, DTS and its allied Bible schools continued to instruct thousands of rank-and-file Baptists and to introduce them to the expanding world of interdenominational evangelicalism.

After its exclusion from the PCUS and PCUSA in the early to mid-1940s, DTS experienced a shift in the denominational background of its student body and the career paths of its graduates. By the late 1940s, independents and Baptists exceeded the number of Presbyterians studying at DTS. As a result, the seminary emerged as a major training center for independent churches and interdenominational parachurch agencies.[58] Many southern evangelicals influenced by the nondenominational fundamentalist movement chose to retain their denominational affiliation, but others separated from the South's traditional churches and affiliated more closely with the movement by starting or joining independent Bible churches, a phenomenon that has received no attention from historians of southern religion.[59]

After World War II, the nascent Bible church movement in the South experienced extraordinary growth, much of it due to DTS graduates. A variety of circumstances led to the founding of these independent churches, but one central motivation stood out. Without going into great detail, an overwhelming majority of southern evangelicals entered the Bible church movement because of the same attraction that led so many of their predecessors to attend Bible conferences in the decades prior to World War II—an attraction to dispensationalism and to the expository, didactic style of preaching that characterized DTS professors and alumni. Bible church membership consisted primarily of middle-class Protestants formerly affiliated with the South's mainline evangelical churches. They sought to fulfill the Great Commission through independent faith mission organizations and chiefly turned to DTS and the independent Bible schools for ministerial staff. Reflecting their northern Bible conference roots, these congregations substituted the southern evangelical revival service with an annual Bible conference. Normally, these congregations did not take up an offering during their worship services and specifically rejected the notion of tithing, which they believed related to Israel and the Mosaic Law but not to New Testament churches. Members and visitors were encouraged to give as they "felt led" and to place their offerings in a designated receptacle in the foyer.[60]

These nondenominational churches, together with DTS, the independent Bible schools, and a variety of independent parachurch agencies, represented a distinctive, and virtually unrecognized, northern style of evangelical Christianity in the South. This subculture within southern evangelicalism continues to prosper in the twenty-first century.[61] The controversies surrounding its emergence and growth in the region highlight the movement's divergence from a regional norm. But also exposed is the permeable border that existed between northern and southern evangelical religious beliefs and practices in the late nineteenth and early twentieth centuries and how northern incursions into the South contributed to the varieties of southern evangelicalism.[62]

Conclusion
The Very Civil Convictions of Ed Harrell

Beth Barton Schweiger

A few years ago, I arrived at the Disciples of Christ Historical Society in Nashville to research the early printing work of Alexander Campbell. After announcing my intentions, the woman behind the desk asked, "And are you a Disciple?" I hesitated. If I admitted that I was not, would I be allowed in? In a split second, I made my decision. "No," I said, "but I do know Ed Harrell!"

Given Harrell's anti-institutional convictions, I'm not certain she was impressed. (Although she did admit me into the library.) But my impulse to name him shows that Harrell is the rare historian who can stand in the broad (and to some minds, unbridgeable) gap between the world of professional history and the confessional world of the receptionist at the Disciples' Historical Society. The essays in this collection demonstrate unquestionably that Harrell's presence and his work have enriched those in both worlds. His writing has held a special meaning for those like myself who try to keep a foot planted in each sphere, both academia and church. In what follows, I briefly consider how Harrell's work has extended our understanding of the history of religion in the American South before turning to what I view as a fascinating anomaly in his thought. Although a primitivist of firmest conviction, Harrell is deeply curious about people who are quite different from himself. He has no doubt that he knows the truth, but he remains remarkably interested in the views and experiences of people he flatly believes are wrong about the things that matter most in life. While primitivism and curiosity seem to sit easily enough together in Harrell's thought, this odd pairing sets him apart from his own tradition and (perhaps more surprisingly) from the liberal academic world in which he made his career. Although his ability to hold these views in tension has likely prevented him from resting easily in either church or academy, it is this quality that has allowed him to benefit both.

The great gift of Harrell's work is to remind us that the world is wider than our histories have imagined it to be. In particular, Harrell's insistence that the universe of religious denominations in the South extended far beyond the mainline groups that have dominated the literature has challenged those who see "Southern Evangelicalism" as a monolithic mix of white Baptist, Methodist, and Presbyterian inclinations. He has devoted many pages to describing groups that have been largely ignored by other scholars, mainly, I suspect, because they have never heard of them. Churches of Christ; Free Will Baptists; Pentecostal Fire Baptized Holiness churches; Cumberland Presbyterians; Regular Baptists; the Church of God of Prophecy; New Testament Holiness; Church of God of the Mountain Assembly, Inc.; Emmanuel Holiness church; and the Jesus church—all of these and many others have appeared in Harrell's works. Some of these churches have a formidable tradition of recording their own history. My brief foray into the archives of the early Disciples taught me that the heirs of Campbell and Stone are invariably careful students of their own tradition, but those outside of their ranks have only rarely read their insights. In Harrell's capable hands, we learn how seriously church members took the sectarian debates that left the purportedly "evangelical South" riven with controversy and conflict from the beginning. I was recently reminded of the importance of his work at the death of Oral Roberts, when every obituary I read quoted Harrell's definitive biography of the evangelist.

The location of Roberts's university in northeastern Oklahoma suggests the importance of place to Harrell's work. Like Homer Hailey's family, the people in Harrell's books trekked ever westward, scattering from the Ohio Valley and the Appalachians across the Mississippi, through the Arkansas and Red River valleys, the Ouachita and Ozark Mountains, the Piney Woods of East Texas, and across the Llano Estacado. They tended to settle in places for which others had little use, particularly the stark, windswept counties near the one hundredth meridian. In this, of course, people in the Disciples' tradition were taking part in a much larger national migration, and Harrell has admirably stressed that the Disciples' tradition has always been, as he suggested in the title of his first book, about the larger meaning of America.

Geography has also been central to Harrell's work because of his pioneering focus on the social context of the movements he has studied. Like the Nazarene historian Timothy L. Smith, Harrell anticipated scholarly interest in the sociology and anthropology of religion, and like Smith, he was keen to find significance in the lives of ordinary people. Oddly for a self-declared primitivist, Harrell does not view ideas as the primary movers in history. Instead, he is most fascinated by the context in which people live out their beliefs and has been particularly sensitive to the role of social class in sparking schism. In this sense, Harrell's entire body of work can be viewed as an eloquent reply to H. Richard Niebuhr's *Social Sources of Denominationalism.* He shares Niebuhr's dark view that Christians' compromise with the world resulted in a steep fall from their original mission to proclaim a new, unified humanity without regard to Greek or Jew. Both men know that Christian disunity is sinful. And like Niebuhr, Harrell was convinced that the roots of this disunity lay in the inability to overcome national, racial, and economic conflicts within Christian community. For both men, theology is always grounded in social practice. "Theological opinions have their roots in the relationship of religious life to the cultural and political conditions prevailing in any group of Christians," Niebuhr wrote.[1] There are less complicated ways to understand the history of religion; as Harrell has found, the social context of theology offers no easy answers. "God has been on every side of every social issue I have ever studied; He has participated in every war on every side; He is a Democrat and a Republican, high tariff and low tariff, a fascist and a communist," Harrell has observed.[2]

These similarities belie a huge difference between Niebuhr's and Harrell's account of the past. Harrell has no patience with Niebuhr's Reformed view that the task of the church is to reform the world, that Christ has an interest in transforming culture. (He presumably also disagrees with Niebuhr's view that the early Disciples could be described simply as a "frontier faith.") The world, Harrell explains in history after history of contentious and controversial saints, will always refuse reformation. Nor, he believes, is compromise possible for those who know the truth. As such, schism becomes both the source of, and the antidote for, Christian disunity. "Few themes in the Bible recur more often than the plaintive pleas to 'come out from among them, and be ye separate,'" Harrell wrote in a regular column for a Church of Christ periodical he pointedly titled "Christ versus Culture."[3]

Equally important as the uniqueness of the subjects Harrell has taken up is his generosity toward the people about whom he writes. This generosity stands, remarkably and unapologetically, alongside his flat conviction that those who disagree with his religious views are wrong. "I believe that the individual who rejects the truth which is clear to me will be lost," he wrote in 1967.[4] This conviction is rooted deeply in the theistic commonsense philosophy that persuaded restorationists like Campbell and Stone (and many others) in the wake of the American revolution and has been at the center of the tradition's belief and practice ever since. The Churches of Christ were built on the proposition that a literal reading of the Bible is necessary to salvation.

And yet this starkly exclusionist view is balanced by Harrell's openness to and interest in those who disagree with him. "One of the perverse assumptions of my life," he has written, "is that every man's belief, however curious, deserves consideration."[5] "Perverse," perhaps, because very few of those in his tradition share his deep curiosity about those outside of the Churches of Christ. Harrell devoted years to carefully researching and writing about the pentecostal Oral Roberts, for example, a figure who was not admired by Harrell's own tradition. In this dedication to his craft, his openness to those with whom he disagrees, and his insistence that every life matters, Harrell brings to mind Karl Barth's proclamation that "history is not a paint-box at the disposal of anyone who thinks he knows something and has a need to make his knowledge more impressive . . . history is made up of living men whose work is handed over defenceless to our understanding and appreciation upon their death. Precisely because of this, they have a claim on our courtesy, a claim that their own concerns should be heard and that they should not be used simply as a means to our ends."[6] It seems to me that Harrell's work meets the high standard that Barth laid out.

It is this unusual juxtaposition of primitivist certainty with openness and curiosity that I admire the most about Harrell. In my view, this unusual combination of perspectives is what has enabled him to serve both his church and his colleagues in history well. As Richard Hughes remarked, he understands precisely who he is, and in a strange way, the strength of his own views and his certainty of how history will end allows for this generosity. "I feel comfortable in the presence of conviction, right or wrong," he has observed. "I understand it; and I like it."[7] Harrell easily (and unselfconsciously) calls himself a fanatic. Such a stance is as rare as it is remarkable in the context of the academy in which he has made his career. While the university prides itself on its tolerance, Harrell's convictions have proven too much for some of his peers. The Unitarian Sidney Mead, upon learning that Harrell did not vote, protested that he found this incomprehensible, and declared it to be immoral.[8]

The liberal academy, it seems, does not cotton to a biblical literalist in its ranks, even one who reads Sigmund Freud. In a remarkable early essay published in 1967, the breadth of Harrell's thought about religious belief appears to lead him toward relativism. "Religion is a delusion," he admitted, agreeing with a passage from Freud's *Civilization and Its Discontents.* "It is an admission of human fallibility, an acceptance of defeat, a surrender to the overpowering compulsion to know the unknown, a tranquilizer to still the fear of death . . . it is a product of man's unreasonable insistence that his life have some higher meaning."[9] Different types of people have different religious needs, Harrell explained, because they have different psychological responses to their life experiences. Here we can see his work in plain view: Harrell has been interested in describing the many forms that this "delusion" has taken in human experience. The sectarian Protestants he studied responded to the poverty, sorrow, and hardship in their lives with humility. Economic stability and comfort, by contrast, most often produced religious complacence among Protestant liberals, in his view. "There is no question in my mind but that this is the nature of the sociological division of the Disciples in the nineteenth century," and the basis for twentieth-century rifts between the Disciples and the Churches of Christ, he wrote.[10] Nor is there any doubt whose side he is on. Legalism of the kind he embraces, he argues, happens to be the property of the "psychologically fervent, religiously intense, and socially and economically dispossessed."[11] But just when the broad (and seemingly liberal) implications of this reasoning move toward the conclusion that truth might be found in different Christian traditions, Harrell pulls back. He cannot, he says, explain why the legalistic conservative views he has embraced are true, but he does not need to. "I choose to believe and I do believe."[12]

Harrell's primitivist certainty about the truth of things, then, grants him a peculiar intellectual freedom. It unleashes his expansive curiosity and frees him to exercise a generous understanding toward his subjects, however misinformed they might be. He has no stake at all in proving them wrong, he is simply interested in explaining how they came to be and what they did in this life. In this, he has more freedom and curiosity than his conservative peers in the Churches of Christ, and more tolerance and generosity than his liberal peers in academia. It is hardly surprising that he has not found complete rest in either world. Everything for Harrell the historian turns on understanding, which he views as the chief task of his craft. While the higher work of his immortal soul is to find salvation "through literal obedience to the word of God," the task of the mortal historian is understanding, which holds out the prospect of peace, or at least, of somehow dulling human strife. "If we could attain the lower good of understanding why [humans come to different views of God], the insight would serve us well in our struggle in this life," he concludes.[13] Ed Harrell has offered countless readers the possibility of understanding better the peculiar men and women in his books. There is no better legacy for a historian.

Notes

Chapter 1

1. David Edwin Harrell Jr., *Quest for a Christian America: The Disciples of Christ and American Society to 1866* (Nashville: Disciples of Christ Historical Society, 1966), and idem, *Sources of Division in the Disciples of Christ, 1865–1900* (Atlanta and Athens, GA: Publishing Systems, 1973).

2. David Edwin Harrell Jr., *The Churches of Christ in the Twentieth Century: Homer Hailey's Personal Journey of Faith* (Tuscaloosa: The University of Alabama Press, 2000).

3. David Edwin Harrell Jr., *All Things Are Possible: The Healing and Charismatic Revivals in Modern America* (Bloomington: Indiana University Press, 1975).

4. David Edwin Harrell Jr., *Oral Roberts: An American Life* (Bloomington: Indiana University Press, 1985).

5. David Edwin Harrell Jr., *Pat Robertson: A Personal, Religious, and Political Portrait* (San Francisco: Harper and Row, 1987).

6. David Edwin Harrell Jr., *White Sects and Black Men in the Recent South* (Nashville: Vanderbilt University Press, 1971).

7. David Edwin Harrell Jr., ed., *Varieties of Southern Evangelicalism* (Macon, GA: Mercer University Press, 1981).

8. David Edwin Harrell Jr., "Peculiar People: A Rationale for Modern Conservative Disciples," the Reed Lectures for 1966, in *Disciples and the Church Universal,* ed. Robert O. Fife, David Edwin Harrell Jr., and Ronald E. Osborn (Nashville: Disciples of Christ Historical Society, 1967).

9. David Edwin Harrell Jr., "Recovering the Underside of Southern Religion," in *Autobiographical Reflections on Southern Religious History,* ed. John B. Boles (Athens: University of Georgia Press, 2001), 39–52.

10. Harrell, *The Churches of Christ in the Twentieth Century.*

11. David Edwin Harrell Jr. et al., *Unto a Good Land: A History of the American People* (Grand Rapids, MI: William B. Eerdmans, 2005).

12. Harrell, *Quest for a Christian America.*

13. David Edwin Harrell Jr., "Walter Scott and the Nineteenth-Century Evangelical Spirit," in *Walter Scott: A Nineteenth-Century Evangelical,* ed. Mark A. Toulouse (St. Louis: Chalice Press, 1999), 35.

14. Harrell, *Oral Roberts.*

15. Harrell, *Pat Robertson.*

16. Edward Burnett Tylor, *Primitive Culture: Researches into the Development of Mythology, Philosophy, Religion, Art, and Custom,* 2 vols. (London: John Murray, 1871).

Chapter 2

1. George Floyd Taylor, *The Spirit and the Bride* (Dunn, NC: By the author, 1907), 90–96. The biblical reference for stages of rainfall as a sign of God's restoration is Joel 2:23.

2. James R. Goff Jr. and Grant Wacker, *Portraits of a Generation: Early Pentecostal Leaders* (Fayetteville: University of Arkansas Press, 2002), xi.

3. Augustus Cerillo Jr. and Grant Wacker, "Bibliography and Historiography of Pentecostalism in the United States," in *The New International Dictionary of Pentecostal and Charismatic Movements,* ed. Stanley M. Burgess, rev. and exp. ed. (Grand Rapids, MI: Zondervan, 2002), 382.

4. Charles William Shumway, "A Study of 'The Gift of Tongues'" (AB thesis, University of Southern California, 1914); and "A Critical History of Glossolalia" (PhD diss., Boston University, 1919).

5. Bennett F. Lawrence, *The Apostolic Faith Restored* (St. Louis: Gospel Publishing House, 1916); Stanley H. Frodsham, *With Signs Following* (Springfield, MO: Gospel Publishing House, 1926); Donald Gee, *The Pentecostal Movement* (London: Elim Publishing, 1949); Joseph Enoch Campbell, *The Pentecostal Holiness Church, 1898–1948* (Franklin Springs, GA: Pentecostal Holiness Church Press, 1951); Ethel E. Goss, *The Winds of God: The Story of the Early Pentecostal Days (1901–1914) in the Life of Howard A. Goss* (New York: Comet Press Books, 1958); and John Thomas Nichol, *Pentecostalism* (New York: Harper and Row, 1966).

6. Vinson Synan, *The Holiness-Pentecostal Movement in the United States* (Grand Rapids, MI: William B. Eerdman's, 1971); William W. Menzies, *Anointed to Serve: The Story of the Assemblies of God* (Springfield, MO: Gospel Publishing House, 1971); Edith Lydia Waldvogel, "The 'Overcoming Life': A Study in the Reformed Evangelical Origins of Pentecostalism" (PhD diss., Harvard University, 1977); and Grant Wacker, "The Functions of Faith in Primitive Pentecostalism," *Harvard Theological Review* 77 (1984): 353–75; and "The Pentecostal Tradition," in *Caring and Curing: Health and Medicine in the Western Religious Traditions,* ed. Ronald L. Numbers and Darrel W. Amundsen (New York: Macmillan, 1985), 514–38.

7. David E. Harrell Jr., *All Things Are Possible: The Healing and Charismatic Revivals in Modern America* (Bloomington: Indiana University Press, 1975), ix.

8. Mary L. Schneider, "Are All Things Really Possible?" *Reviews in American History* 5 (March 1977): 118.

9. William C. Martin, "Review of *All Things Are Possible: The Healing and Charismatic Revivals in Modern America*," *Journal of Southern History* 42 (November 1976): 604.

10. Schneider, "Are All Things Really Possible?" 122.

11. Martin, "Review," 603.

12. Paul A. Carter, "Review of *All Things Are Possible: The Healing and Charismatic Revivals in Modern America*," *Journal of American History* 63 (December 1976): 760.

13. Grant Wacker, "Review of *All Things Are Possible: The Healing and Charismatic Revivals in Modern America*," *Church History* 45 (September 1976): 397.

14. Martin, "Review," 604.

15. Ernest R. Sandeen, "Review of *All Things Are Possible: The Healing and Charismatic Revivals in Modern America*," *American Historical Review* 81 (October 1976): 1004.

16. Edwin S. Gaustad, "Review of *Oral Roberts: An American Life*," *Journal of American History* 72 (March 1986): 951.

17. William Martin, "Review of *Oral Roberts: An American Life*," *Journal of Southern History* 53 (February 1987): 135.

18. "Oral Roberts Biography," Oral Roberts University, http://www.oru.edu/oral-roberts/oralroberts.php, accessed July 20, 2011.

Chapter 3

1. David Edwin Harrell Jr., *Quest for a Christian America: The Disciples of Christ and American Society to 1866* (Nashville: Disciples of Christ Historical Society, 1966).

2. David Edwin Harrell Jr., "The Sectional Origins of the Churches of Christ," *Journal of Southern History* 30 (August 1964): 277.

3. David Edwin Harrell Jr., "Peculiar People: A Rationale for Modern Conservative Disciples," the Reed Lectures for 1966, in *Disciples and the Church Universal*, ed. Robert O. Fife, David Edwin Harrell Jr., and Ronald E. Osborn (Nashville: Disciples of Christ Historical Society, 1967), 34–35.

4. Many of the papers from that conference appeared in the *Journal of the American Academy of Religion* 44 (March 1976).

5. Harrell said that he had voted in 1964, casting his ballot against presidential candidate Barry M. Goldwater.

6. David Edwin Harrell Jr., *The Churches of Christ in the Twentieth Century: Homer Hailey's Personal Journey of Faith* (Tuscaloosa: The University of Alabama Press, 2000), 163.

7. Samuel S. Hill Jr., "David Edwin Harrell Jr.: American Religious Historian," *Restoration Quarterly* 46 (Third/Fourth Quarter 2004): 232. Hill made this presentation at a special conference on "Scholarship in Churches of Christ" held in conjunction with the annual meeting of the American Academy of Religion/Society of Biblical Literature, Atlanta, Georgia, November 2003.

8. Hill, "David Edwin Harrell Jr.: American Religious Historian," 229.

9. Harrell, *The Churches of Christ in the Twentieth Century,* 278.

10. Ibid., xv.

11. Ibid., 168.

12. Ibid., 174.

13. David Edwin Harrell Jr., "Epilogue," in *The American Quest for the Primitive Church,* ed. Richard T. Hughes (Urbana: University of Illinois Press, 1988), 244.

14. The refusal of Churches of Christ to take their own history seriously grew from their conviction that they had restored the primitive church of the apostolic age and were indebted, therefore, only to Jesus and the apostles. On this theme, see Richard T. Hughes, *Reclaiming a Heritage: Reflections on the Heart, Soul, and Future of Churches of Christ* (Abilene, TX: ACU Press, 2002), 46–53.

15. Harrell, *The Churches of Christ in the Twentieth Century,* 44.

16. Ibid., 374.

17. Harrell, "Epilogue," 241.

18. Harrell, "Peculiar People," 40–41.

19. Harrell, "Epilogue," 244–45.

Chapter 4

1. John B. Boles, "The Discovery of Southern Religious History," in *Interpreting Southern History: Historiographical Essays in Honor of Sanford W. Higginbotham,* ed. John B. Boles and Evelyn Thomas Nolen (Baton Rouge: Louisiana State University Press, 1987), 511–14.

2. Beth Barton Schweiger and Donald Mathews, eds., *Religion in the American South: Protestants and Others in History and Culture* (Chapel Hill: University of North Carolina Press, 2004).

3. David Edwin Harrell Jr., "Recovering the Underside of Southern Religion," in *Autobiographical Reflections on Southern Religious History,* ed. John B. Boles (Athens: University of Georgia Press, 2001), 39.

4. Ibid., 39–42.

5. John Lee Eighmy, *Churches in Cultural Captivity: A History of the Social Attitudes of Southern Baptists* (Knoxville: University of Tennessee Press, 1972).

6. Boles, "Discovery of Southern Religious History," 511–14.

7. David Edwin Harrell Jr., *White Sects and Black Men in the Recent South* (Nashville: Vanderbilt University Press, 1971); Boles, "Discovery of Southern Religious History," xvi.

8. Norman Lederer, "Review of *White Sects and Black Men in the Recent South* by David Edwin Harrell Jr.," *The Alabama Review* 34 (October 1972): 241–42.

9. Harrell, *White Sects;* Boles, "Discovery of Southern Religious History," 522–23.

10. David Edwin Harrell Jr., *Quest for a Christian America: The Disciples of Christ*

and American Society to 1866 (Nashville: Disciples of Christ Historical Society, 1966); and *The Social Sources of Division in the Disciples of Christ* (Atlanta and Athens, GA: Publishing Systems, 1973); Walter B. Posey, "Review of *The Social Sources of Division of the Disciples of Christ, 1865–1900,* by David Edwin Harrell Jr.," *Journal of Southern History* 40 (November 1974): 678–79.

11. Harrell, "Recovering the Underside of American Religion," 44.

12. Ibid., 45.

13. Ibid., 47; William Martin, "Review of *All Things Are Possible,* by David Edwin Harrell Jr.," *Journal of Southern History* 42 (November 1976): 678–79.

14. Wayne Flynt, "Review of *Pat Robertson,* by David Edwin Harrell Jr.," *Georgia Historical Quarterly* 72 (Fall 1988): 583–85.

15. Harrell, "Recovering the Underside of American Religion," 49.

16. David Edwin Harrell Jr., *The Churches of Christ in the Twentieth Century: Homer Hailey's Personal Journey of Faith* (Tuscaloosa: The University of Alabama Press, 2000).

17. Harrell, "Recovering the Underside of Southern Religion," 43.

18. Harrell, *Churches of Christ in the Twentieth Century,* xii.

19. Harrell, "Recovering the Underside of Southern Religion," 43.

Chapter 5

1. Sherry Andrews, "Keeping the Faith," *Charisma* 7 (October 1981): 24–30.

2. Defining the terms used in this study, such as *pentecostal* and *charismatic,* is a difficult task since they have many nuances and there is no consensus either among scholars or the participants about their meaning. Pentecostals and charismatics are most often identified by their belief in the miraculous gifts of the Holy Spirit, especially glossolalia ("speaking in tongues") and divine healing. The ecstatic experience of speaking in tongues is, according to pentecostals and charismatics, the evidence of "being filled with the Holy Spirit" or "receiving the baptism of the Holy Spirit." I use the term *pentecostal* when referring to those who belong to traditional pentecostal denominations such as the Assemblies of God and the Church of God in Christ (COGIC). I typically use *charismatic* when referring to those who are not members of an established denomination or those who belong to non-pentecostal denominations, such as Baptists and Methodists. The term *neo-pentecostal* is used to identify mainline congregations that have adopted pentecostal and charismatic theology and worship styles. Some of these churches remained in their traditional denominations while others became independent, effectively becoming charismatic churches.

3. Vinson Synan, *The Holiness-Pentecostal Tradition: Charismatic Movements in the Twentieth Century,* 2d ed. (1971; Grand Rapids, MI: William B. Eerdmans, 1997), 223–24; David Edwin Harrell Jr., *All Things Are Possible: The Healing and Charismatic Revivals in Modern America* (Bloomington: Indiana University Press, 1975), 135–49, 225–33.

4. David Edwin Harrell Jr., *Oral Roberts: An American Life* (Bloomington: Indiana University Press, 1985), vii.

5. Oral Roberts, *Expect a Miracle: My Life and Ministry* (Nashville: Thomas Nelson Publishers, 1995), 231–32.

6. Andrews, "Keeping the Faith," 24–30; Harrell, *All Things Are Possible,* 185–86; "Obituary—Rev. Kenneth E. Hagin," http://www.rhema.org/obituary.cfm, accessed December 15, 2004.

7. "A Great Heritage of Faith—You're Still a Part of the Vision!" *Connections* 26 (Winter 2001): 2–3; Harrell, *All Things Are Possible,* 136, 185–86; Andrews, "Keeping the Faith," 24–30; Kenneth E. Hagin, "Looking to the Future," *Word of Faith* (*WF*) 19 (September 1986): 2–5.

8. Kenneth Hagin Jr., "Trend toward Faith Movement," *Charisma* 11 (August 1985): 67–70.

9. Stanley M. Burgess, ed., and Eduard M. Van Der Maas, assoc. ed., *The New International Dictionary of Pentecostal and Charismatic Movements,* rev. ed. (Grand Rapids, MI: Zondervan, 2002), s.v. "Positive Confession"; Heather L. Landrus, "Hearing 3 John 2 in the Voices of History," a paper presented at the annual meeting of the Society for Pentecostal Studies, Tulsa, Oklahoma, March 2001.

10. "Rhema Bible Training Center," *Charisma* (October 1981): 30.

11. Andrews, "Keeping the Faith," 24–30; Kenneth Hagin Jr., interview by David Edwin Harrell Jr., March 29, 2001, Tulsa, Oklahoma.

12. "Rhema Bible Training Center," 30–31.

13. Kenneth E. Hagin and Kenneth Hagin Jr., interview by David Edwin Harrell Jr., December 12, 1983. Some of his harshest critics included Hank Hannegraff, *Christianity in Crisis* (Eugene, OR: Harvest House Publishers, 1997); David Hunt and T. A. McMahon, *The Seduction of Christianity* (Eugene, OR: Harvest House Publishers, 1985); D. R. McConnell, *A Different Gospel* (Peabody, MA: Hendrickson Publishers, 1988); John Ankerberg and John Weldon, *The Facts on the Faith Movement* (Eugene, OR: Harvest House Publishers, 1993); Michael Horton, ed., *The Agony of Deceit* (Chicago: Moody Press, 1990); mention of Charles Farah in Andrews, "Keeping the Faith," 24–30.

14. Andrews, "Keeping the Faith," 24–30.

15. Michael Horton, "The TV Gospel," in *The Agony of Deceit,* 123.

16. Kenneth Hagin Jr., "Trend toward Faith Movement," 67–70; Derek E. Vreeland, "Restructuring Word of Faith Theology: A Defense, Analysis, and Refinement of the Theology of the Word of Faith Movement," paper presented at the annual meeting of the Society for Pentecostal Studies, Tulsa, Oklahoma, March 2001. For a synopsis of positive confession theology see L. Lovett's entry in Burgess, ed., *New International Dictionary,* s.v. "Positive Confession Theology."

17. Hagin, "Trend toward Faith Movement," 67–70; announcements of various events, *WF* 14 (February 1981): 15.

18. "About Joel Osteen," http://www.joelosteen.com/site/PageServer?pagename=AboutJoel, accessed May 18, 2005; "*New York Times* Best Sellers List," http://www.nytimes.com/pages/books/bestseller/index.html, accessed May 18, 2005.

19. Paul Thigpen, "The New Black Charismatics," *Charisma* 16 (November 1990): 58–67.

20. Hagin, "Trend toward Faith Movement," 67–70; comments by friends about Kenneth E. Hagin's fifty years in ministry, *WF* 17 (October 1984): 16; "'Best Campmeeting Ever' Focuses on the Supernatural," *WF* 15 (October 1982): 4–14.

21. Rosie Grier testified about how Price's and Hagin's ministries affected his life, *WF* 14 (October 1981): 6.

22. Price was a popular speaker at Hagin's annual Campmeeting and other RBTC functions. Hagin and Buddy Harrison continued to promote his books and tapes throughout the 1970s and 1980s. See "Behind the Scenes," *WF* 7 (September 1974): 5; *WF* 7 (December 1974): 7; *WF* 8 (March 1975): 8; *WF* 14 (October 1981): 6; "'Best Campmeeting Ever' Focuses on the Supernatural," 4–14; *WF* 18 (October 1985): 13–14; advertisement in *Charisma* 13 (April 1988).

23. Frederick K. C. Price, *Race, Religion, and Racism: A Bold Encounter with Division in the Church*, vol. 1 (Los Angeles: Faith One Publishing, 1999), 31–33.

24. Ibid., 53–61.

25. Billy Bruce, "Fred Price Triggers Debate over Racism," *Charisma* 23 (April 1998): 16–17; Price, *Race, Religion, and Racism*, xiii, 6–7, 41–54.

26. Price, *Race, Religion, and Racism*, 34.

27. Ibid., 23.

28. Ibid., 16.

29. Ibid., 40.

30. Ibid., 35.

31. Ibid., 15–16.

32. Ed Donnally, "He's Still Not Afraid to Confront," *Charisma* 26 (August 2000): 66–69.

33. Bruce, "Fred Price Triggers Debate over Racism," 16–17.

34. Kenneth Hagin Jr., "Take the High Road," *WF* 31 (July 1998): 2.

35. Kenneth Hagin Jr., "What Goes In Is What Comes Out!" *WF* 31 (August 1998): 2; "Overcoming Offense," *WF* 34 (April 2001): 2.

36. Advertisement for Campmeeting 1993 (immediately after the race controversy erupted between Hagin Jr. and Price, four of the featured speakers at Campmeeting were black [Clinton Utterbach, Keith Butler, J. C. Hash Sr., and Jimmie Pierce]), *WF* 26 (April 1993): n.p.; "Rhema Bible Training Center Day," 9; "Winter Bible Seminar '97—A Taste of Heaven on Earth," *WF* 30 (May 1997): 10–12 (quotation); "Word of Faith International Christian Center," http://www.wordoffaith-icc.org/home.htm, accessed April 20, 2001.

37. Summary of Leroy Thompson's message on faith at Campmeeting 1993, *WF* 26

(October 1993): 10–13; summary of Thompson's message at Campmeeting 1994, *WF* 27 (October 1994): 13–14; summary of Butler's and Thompson's messages at Campmeeting 1996, *WF* 29 (October 1996): 12–13; *WF* 30 (October 1997): 19–20; "Campmeeting '98: Fan the Flame," *WF* 31 (October 1998): 13–16; "Ever Increasing Word Ministries," http://www.eiwm.org, accessed March 12, 2001.

38. Dr. Creflo A. Dollar, "How It All Began," *Changing Your World* 3 (August 2001): 6–9.

39. The *Atlanta Journal-Constitution* (*AJC*) documents the struggles Dollar faced with his College Park neighbors as his ministry grew and his facilities expanded. See Barbara Ann Moore, "$6.5 Million Sanctuary-in-the-Round: Church Plans Dome Home: But World Changers' Neighbors Worry," *AJC,* October 10, 1992, sec. B; Barbara Ann Moore, "Megachurch, Residents Square Off: Neighborhood Opposes Expansion," *AJC,* November 26, 1992, sec. K; Ken Foskett, "'Mega' Church a Cross for Fulton to Bear: County to Consider Religious Freedom, Community Needs," *AJC,* February 3, 1993, sec. C; Kent Kimes, "Dome of Contention: Residents Resist Church Plan: World Changers Wants to Expand Its Building," *AJC,* October 12, 1995, sec. K; Kent Kimes, "College Park Church's Fight with Neighbors, County Grows," *AJC,* October 26, 1995, sec. K; Kent Kimes, "Neighborhood vs. Church: Commission Postpones Request for Expansion," *AJC,* November 9, 1995, sec. K; Kent Kimes, "Megachurch Wins Expansion Approval after Protest Folds," *AJC,* December 14, 1995, sec. I; Kent Kimes, "Neighborhood Leader Draws Fire for Backing Church Expansion," *AJC,* December 21, 1995, sec. K; Kent Kimes, "World Changers Make a Sort of Peace with Dome's Opponent's," *AJC,* January 4, 1996, sec. I; Kay S. Pedrotti, "Ministry Gets Planners' Nod for New Site Rezoning," *AJC,* April 24, 1997, sec. K; Sandra Eckstein, "Neighbors Fear the Impact of Megachurch's Expansion," *AJC,* May 17, 2000, sec. B; John McCosh, "Parking Ticket: Church Expansion Curbed Zoning: A Megachurch was Pushed and Pulled over New Facility, and Fulton Planners Voted No," *AJC,* May 18, 2000, sec. C; Sandra Eckstein, "Fulton Panel Kills Church Complex," *AJC,* June 8, 2000, sec. B; "Rezoning Denied for Large Church," *AJC,* June 15, 2000; Charles Yoo, "Church Gets More Parking," *AJC,* November 20, 2001, sec. E.

40. Vicki Jamison-Peterson, *El Shaddai: The God of More Than Enough!* (Tulsa: Vicki Jamison-Peterson Ministries, 1983), 5–10.

41. Vicki Jamison-Peterson, *How You Can Have Joy,* rev. ed. (Tulsa: Vicki Jamison-Peterson Ministries, 1985), 13; Vicki Jamison, "The Healing Power of the Mind," *It's a New Day* (September 1976): 2–3; Vicki Jamison, "Wonderful! The Name of Jesus," *It's a New Day* (May 1976): 2.

42. Sharon Burton, "The Name of Jesus," *It's a New Day* (May 1976): 1, 4; Jamison-Peterson, *El Shaddai,* 84–86; Vicki Jamison, "Great Things He Hath Done," *It's a New Day* special edition (Spring 1977): 1–4.

43. "Billye Brim's Biography," http://www.billyebrim.com/, accessed July 28, 2001; Billye Brim, "The *POWER* in the BLOOD of JESUS," *Glorious Connections* (Spring

1994): 2; Billye Brim, report on Migdal Arbel, LTD, Prayer Mountain in the Galilee, June 2000, sent to author by Billye Brim Ministries, summer 2002; Billye Brim, "The Jews, The Nations, The Church," *Glorious Connections* (September 1989): n.p.; Billye Brim, "The Purpose of Prayer Mountain in the Ozarks," promotional brochure sent to author by Billye Brim Ministries, summer 2002; Billye Brim, "God's Glorious Connections," *Glorious Connections* (November 1986): n.p.

44. Lynette Hagin, "The Four 'F's of Bearing Fruit," *WF* 31 (March 1998): 26–28; "Lynette Hagin Named Director of RHEMA," *WF* 15 (August 1982): 9; "Kindle the Flame Women's Conference," *WF* 34 (February 2001): 21–22.

45. "We're Preparing Laborers To Reap the Precious Fruit of the Earth," *WF* 19 (June 1986): 8–9; Kenneth E. Hagin, "Looking to the Future," *WF* 19 (September 1986): 2–5; comments by friends about Hagin's fifty years in ministry, *WF* 17 (October 1984): 15–17; Kenneth Hagin Jr., "Trend toward Faith Movement," 67–70; Andrews, "Keeping the Faith," 24–30; Harrell, *All Things Are Possible,* 186; "Campmeeting '98: Fan the Flame," *WF* 31 (October 1998): 13–16; "Campmeeting 2000: So Much More Than You've Seen Before," *WF* 33 (October 2000): 12–14, 16, 18; Burgess, ed., *New International Dictionary,* s.v. "Hagin, Kenneth E."; Jeff Dunn, "Faith That Just Won't Stop," *Charisma* 26 (August 2000): 70–71; "The Ministry behind the Ministry," *WF* 22 (September 1989): 9; Kenneth E. Hagin, interview by David Edwin Harrell Jr., May 24, 1973, Birmingham, Alabama.

46. "We're Preparing Laborers to Reap the Precious Fruit of the Earth," 8–9; "A Great Heritage of Faith—You're Still a Part of the Vision!," 2 (quotation); "Rhema Bible Training Center: 'The Anointing Makes the Difference,'" *WF* 19 (May 1986): 8–11; "Lynette Hagin Named Director of RHEMA," 9; "Rhema Bible Training Center," 30–31; "RBTC Updates," *Connections* 26 (Winter 2001): 10; Hagin, "Trend toward Faith Movement," 67–70; "Graduation '92: A Gateway to the Nations!" *WF* 25 (July 1992): 8–9; "Be a Vessel Yielded unto God!" *WF* 31 (July 1998): 9–11; Kenneth Hagin Jr., interview by David Edwin Harrell Jr., March 29, 2001, Tulsa, Oklahoma.

47. "RHEMA Bible Training Center: Preparing the Way of the Lord!" *WF* 20 (June 1987): 2–4.

48. David Beebe, "Where Do You Fit In?" *Connections* 26 (Winter 2001): 2.

49. "RHEMA Bible Training Center: Preparing the Way of the Lord!" 2–4; "Campmeeting 1999: For Such a Time as This," *WF* 32 (October 1999): 4–7; "Nations News: Taking Rhema to the World!" *Connections* 26 (Winter 2001): 6–8; "Nations News: Taking Rhema to the World!" *Connections* 26 (Winter 2001): 6.

50. Norimitsu Onishi, "Africans Fill Churches That Celebrate Wealth," *New York Times on the Web,* Wednesday, March 13, 2002, www.nytimes.com/2002/03/13/international/africa/12NIGE.html, accessed March 13, 2002.

51. Ibid.

52. "A Great Heritage of Faith—You're Still a Part of the Vision!" *Connections* 26 (Winter 2001): 2–3; "Nations News: Taking Rhema to the World!" 6–8; Ken Walker,

"Twenty People Who Touched Our Lives," *Charisma* (August 1995): 37–41; Dunn, "Faith That Just Won't Stop," 70–71; Kenneth Hagin Jr., interview by David Edwin Harrell Jr., March 29, 2001, Tulsa, Oklahoma.

53. "Third Generation Hagin Enters Ministry," *WF* 24 (October 1991): 16; Dunn, "Faith That Just Won't Stop," 70–71.

54. Mrs. Lynette Hagin, "An Introduction to Our Partners," *WF* 30 (January 1997): 10; "Be a Vessel Yielded unto God!" 9–11.

55. David B. Barrett, founder of the World Evangelization Research Centre and coeditor of the *World Christian Encyclopedia,* provides the most comprehensive statistical analysis of this growth. He asserts that there were roughly half a billion pentecostal, charismatic, and neo-charismatic adherents worldwide at the turn of the twenty-first century. See David B. Barrett, George T. Kurian, and Todd M. Johnson, *World Christian Encyclopedia: A Comparative Survey of Churches and Religions in the Modern World,* 2nd ed. (1982; New York: Oxford University Press, 2001); Burgess, ed., *New International Dictionary,* s.v. "Global Statistics"; David Barrett, "The Worldwide Holy Spirit Renewal," in *The Century of the Holy Spirit: 100 Years of Pentecostal and Charismatic Renewal, 1901–2001,* ed. Vinson Synan (Nashville: Thomas Nelson Publishers, 2001).

56. Kate Bowler, "From Far and Wide: The Canadian Faith Movement," Church, Christianity.ca, http://www.christianity.ca/NetCommunity/Page.aspx?pid=7187, accessed December 14, 2010; Simon Coleman, "Conservative Protestantism and the World Order: The Faith Movement in the United States and Sweden," *Sociology of Religion* 54 (Winter 1993): 353–73, http://www.jstor.org/stable/3711779, accessed December 15, 2010; Kirk R. MacGregor, "The Word of Faith Movement: A Theological Conflation of the Nation of Islam and Mormonism?" *Journal of the American Academy of Religion* 75 (Spring 2007): 87–120, http://jaar.oxfordjournals.org/, accessed December 14, 2010; David Maxwell, "'Delivered from the Spirit of Poverty?': Pentecostalism, Prosperity, and Modernity in Zimbabwe," *Journal of Religion in Africa* 28 (August 1998): 350–73, http://www.jstor.org/stable/1581574, accessed December 15, 2010; Joel Robbins, "The Globalization of Pentecostal and Charismatic Christianity," *Annual Review of Anthropology* 33 (2004): 117–43, http://www.jstor.org/stable/25064848, accessed December 15, 2010.

Chapter 6

1. Associated Press, "U.S. Evangelists Stoned in Italy; Charge That Priests Incited Mobs," *New York Times,* January 8, 1950. B. C. Goodpasture (BCG), "Our Brethren Persecuted By Catholics in Italy," *Gospel Advocate* (*GA*), January 19, 1950. BCG, "Catholic Pressure Closes Orphan Home," *GA,* January 26, 1950. BCG, "The Situation in Italy," *GA,* March 9, 1950. Orville McDonald, "Report of Trip to Rome," no date (probably 1951), Reuel Lemmons Papers, Box 1, Center for Restoration Studies, Brown Library, Abilene Christian University, Abilene, Texas.

2. Associated Press, "U.S. Evangelists Stoned in Italy; Charge That Priests Incited Mobs." M. Norvel Young, "Why We Are Being Persecuted in Italy," *GA*, February 2, 1950.

3. Cled E. Wallace, "That Rock Fight in Italy," *Gospel Guardian* (*GG*), January 19, 1950. Cled E. Wallace, "Getting Me Straightened Out," *GG*, March 2, 1950.

4. BCG, "The Pope's Back Yard," *GA*, February 16, 1950. BCG, "Editor's Note," appended to Harvey W. Riggs, "Be Wise and Harmless (Matt. 10:16)," *GA*, February 9, 1950.

5. For a succinct overview of the movement, see David Edwin Harrell Jr., "Restorationism and the Stone-Campbell Tradition," in *Encyclopedia of the American Religious Experience*, vol. 2, ed. Charles H. Lippy and Peter W. Williams (New York: Charles Scribner's Sons, 1988), 845–58.

6. Richard T. Hughes, *Reviving the Ancient Faith: The Story of Churches of Christ in America* (Grand Rapids, MI: Eerdmans, 1996), 239, 242.

7. David Edwin Harrell Jr., *The Churches of Christ in the Twentieth Century: Homer Hailey's Personal Journey of Faith* (Tuscaloosa: The University of Alabama Press, 2000), 71–73, 167.

8. Hughes, *Reviving the Ancient Faith*, 233.

9. After battling liberal church figures for several years, fundamentalists lost bids to control denominations like the Northern Baptist Convention and the Presbyterian Church in the U.S.A. In addition, they were mostly unsuccessful in their antievolution crusade. Numerous fundamentalist organizations created soon after World War I in order to fight modernism in the churches and in public life were no longer viable by 1930, and fundamentalism as a national movement was all but dead. See Joel A. Carpenter, *Revive Us Again: The Reawakening of American Fundamentalism* (New York: Oxford University Press, 1997).

10. William Vance Trollinger Jr., *God's Empire: William Bell Riley and Midwestern Fundamentalism* (Madison: University of Wisconsin Press, 1990).

11. Douglas A. Foster, *Will the Cycle Be Unbroken? Churches of Christ Face the 21st Century* (Abilene, TX: ACU Press, 1994), 67–68.

12. Ed Harrell, "B. C. Goodpasture: Leader of Institutional Thought," in *They Being Dead Yet Speak: Florida College Annual Lectures, 1981*, ed. Melvin D. Curry (Temple Terrace: Florida College Bookstore, 1981), 249.

13. Foster, *Will the Cycle Be Unbroken?*, 67.

14. Jesse P. Sewell to Leon B. McQuiddy, undated (probably early 1938), Jesse P. Sewell Papers, University Archives, Brown Library Special Collections, Abilene Christian University, Abilene, Texas.

15. H. Leo Boles to BCG, September 3, 1938, Benton Cordell Goodpasture Papers, Disciples of Christ Historical Society, Nashville (BCG Papers). On the "fighting style," see Hughes, *Reviving the Ancient Faith*, 196.

16. R. L. Whiteside to Leon B. McQuiddy, undated (probably late 1947), transcript in author's possession, original in private hands. R. L. Whiteside, "The Editor," *Bible Banner*, March 1949.

17. Price Billingsley, "Betrayal Plus Bad Business: An Open Letter [to] L. B. McQuiddy," *Apostolic Times,* July 1939. Price Billingsley to BCG, April 1, 1942, and August 9, 1946, BCG Papers. Price Billingsley to Leon B. McQuiddy and BCG, November 7, 1946, BCG Papers.

18. G. C. Brewer to BCG, December 30, 1940, BCG Papers.

19. Fanning Yater Tant (FYT), "Policy of the Gospel Guardian," *Bible Banner,* April 1949. N. B. Hardeman (NBH) to BCG, April 21, 1949, BCG Papers.

20. BCG, "Unstable as Water," *GA,* July 7, 1949.

21. G. C. Brewer to BCG, August 13, 1949, BCG Papers. G. C. Brewer, "What Doctrine Have We Learned with Reference to Schools and Orphan Homes?" *GA,* October 13, 1949.

22. See, for example, Cled E. Wallace, "Is It Growth or Apostasy?" *GG,* June 2, 1949; FYT, "Dawn of a New Era?" *GG,* August 18, 1949; and FYT, "A Hopeful Sign," *GG,* October 6, 1949.

23. Cled E. Wallace, "In the Middle of the Rock Fight," *GG,* February 2, 1950.

24. FYT, "Let Us Study the Question," *GG,* April 6, 1950. Roy E. Cogdill, "Centralized Control and Oversight," *GG,* April 20, 1950. FYT, "Not Alone—We Hope," *GG,* April 20, 1950.

25. Cecil N. Wright, "Cooperation on a Scriptural Basis," *GA,* May 11, 1950. G. C. Brewer, "Missionaries Ready for the Field: Who 'Sponsors' 'Sponsoring'?" *GA,* April 13, 1950. FYT, "The Overflow," *GG,* April 27, 1950. BCG, "More 'Gospel Advocate—1940 Style,'" *GA,* May 4, 1950.

26. BCG, "Another Phenomenon," *GA,* July 17, 1952. BCG, "What I Like about the Churches of Christ," *GA,* June 5, 1952. BCG, "As Others See Us," *GA,* April 24, 1952.

27. On the general postwar "revival," see Martin E. Marty, *Modern American Religion,* vol. 3, *Under God, Indivisible, 1941–1960* (Chicago: University of Chicago Press, 1996), 277–330.

28. Michael Casey, "Church Growth: New Information," parts 1–2, *Image,* May 1 and May 15, 1987.

29. See Robert E. Hooper, *A Distinct People: A History of the Churches of Christ in the 20th Century* (West Monroe, LA: Howard Publishing, 1993), 172–80, 187–90, 284–86; Hughes, *Reviving the Ancient Faith,* 228–35, 239–50, 261–63; Harrell, *The Churches of Christ,* 151–60, 164; and Michael W. Casey, *Saddlebags, City Streets, and Cyberspace: A History of Preaching in the Churches of Christ* (Abilene, TX: ACU Press, 1995), 97.

30. Willard Collins, "A Local Church On the March: Church of Christ, Madison, Tenn." *GA,* October 13, 1955. Ira North, "A Former Student and Faculty Member Tells 'What Lipscomb Means to Me,'" *GA,* May 3, 1951. Ira North, "Let's Be Alive in '55," *GA,* December 23, 1954.

31. Ira North to BCG, postmarked July 26, 1957, BCG Papers.

32. On terminology, see, for example, BCG, "Lipscomb on Cooperation," *GA,* February 15, 1951; BCG, "Problems or Dangers Confronting the Church," transcript,

n.d., 24 pp., BCG Papers; and Wm. E. Wallace, "A Glossary of Terms," *GG*, December 16, 1954.

33. Hughes, *Reviving the Ancient Faith,* 231. BCG, "Diotrephes, Who Loved the Preeminence," *GA,* April 26, 1951. BCG, "How Many Rooms in the Ark?" *GA,* February 10, 1955. BCG, "Here and There," *GA,* May 26, 1955.

34. NBH to BCG, December 21, 1957, and September 9, 1958, BCG Papers. BCG, "Here and There," *GA,* August 1, 1957.

35. William E. Wallace, "A Tributary of Bitterness," *Vanguard,* November 1983.

36. BCG, "Here and There," *GA,* May 10, 1951. BCG, "Religious Papers and Divided Churches," *GA,* June 14, 1951, and July 20, 1933. NBH to BCG, June 1, 1951, BCG Papers. BCG, "The Voice of the Turtle," *GA,* July 12, 1951.

37. FYT, "Cogdill, Lufkin, and Goodpasture," *Vanguard,* February 1984.

38. Noble Patterson and Terry J. Gardner, eds., *Foy E. Wallace Jr.: Soldier of the Cross* (Fort Worth, TX: Wallace Memorial Fund, 1999), 103–6, 289.

39. Roy E. Cogdill, "What Is That to Thee?" *GG,* August 2, 1951. FYT, "An Open Letter to Brother Goodpasture," *GG,* August 2, 1951. BCG, "What Is That to Thee" *GA,* August 23, 1951.

40. FYT, "Re-statement of Convictions," *GG,* September 20, 1951. Roy E. Cogdill, "You Can See What I Meant," *GG,* September 20, 1951.

41. NBH to BCG, October 3, 1951, BCG Papers. Cogdill, "You Can See What I Meant." BCG, "It Is Time to Name the Man," *GA,* November 1, 1951. BCG, "They Want the $25," *GA,* October 25, 1951.

42. BCG, "An Elder Writes," *GA,* November 18, 1954. BCG, "Paul and the Judaizers," *GA,* June 3, 1954.

43. BCG, "They Commend the Elder Who Wrote," *GA,* December 9, 1954.

44. Roy E. Cogdill, "Institutional Pressure Control," *GG,* February 17, 1955. FYT, "On Achieving Unity," *Vanguard,* October 1982. Harrell, *The Churches of Christ,* 143.

45. BCG, "Here and There," *GA,* June 9, 1955. NBH to BCG, December 15, 1954, and March 15 and 29, 1955, BCG Papers.

46. Guy N. Woods, "The Noose Tightens!" *GA,* January 29, 1959. See Guy N. Woods, "Orphanages and Homes for the Aged," *GA,* October 14, 1954; the seven-part series concluded December 16, 1954. E. Claude Gardner, "I Am Optimistic," *GA,* February 27, 1958.

47. Foy E. Wallace Jr., "For General Information," *GA,* November 24, 1955. BCG and John D. Cox, "Organization and Work of the Church," *GA,* August 8, 1957. BCG, "Brother Crouch's Statement," *GA,* July 24, 1958. Batsell Barrett Baxter and M. Norvel Young, eds., *Preachers of Today: A Book of Brief Biographical Sketches and Pictures of Living Gospel Preachers,* vol. 2 (Nashville: Gospel Advocate, 1959), 97. Cogdill, "Institutional Pressure Control."

48. Charles E. Crouch, "A Change of Viewpoint," *GA,* July 24, 1958. Thomas B. Warren, "Anti Reaction to This Is More Strong Evidence That Their Ship Is Sinking," *GA,* October 16, 1958.

49. Roy H. Lanier, "The Middle of the Road," *Firm Foundation,* five consecutive installments beginning February 12, 1957. Reuel Lemmons, "Read Roy Lanier's Articles," *Firm Foundation,* February 12, 1957. Guy N. Woods, "Lanier—In the Middle of the Wrong Road!" *GA,* April 11 and 18, 1957. See correspondence between Woods and Lanier, and Thomas B. Warren and Lemmons, Lemmons Papers, Box 16.

50. Reuel Lemmons, "Is The Home A Divine Institution?" *Firm Foundation,* February 4, 1958. Guy N. Woods, "A Shocking Editorial," *GA,* March 27, 1958. NBH to Violet DeVaney, April 11, 1958, BCG Papers. "Brother Lemmons and the Orphan Homes," *GA,* March 19, 1959. H. A. Dixon, "Firm Foundation's Seventy-Fifth Anniversary," *GA,* March 19, 1959. Reuel Lemmons to BCG, 20 January 1959, BCG Papers.

51. Hughes, *Reviving the Ancient Faith,* 341.

52. Harrell, *The Churches of Christ,* 139.

53. Pat Hardeman, "A Statement of Conviction," *GA,* March 13, 1958. See, for example, Pat Hardeman, "The Gospel Versus Dogmatism," *GA,* August 21, 1958.

54. NBH to BCG, September 9, 1958. BCG, "Concerning Pat Hardeman," *GA,* October 29, 1959.

55. James R. Cope, "Florida Christian College: Retrospect and Prospect," *GA,* July 17, 1958.

56. BCG, "That Florida Christian College Advertisement," *GA,* August 21, 1958. Eddie G. Couch to BCG, August 28, 1958, BCG Papers.

57. BCG, "Twenty Years," *GA,* February 26, 1959. Hughes, *Reviving the Ancient Faith,* 10, 239. John E. Kirk, "A Free Press Under Christ," *GA,* February 10, 1955. James D. Groves, "Send the 'Advocate' This Year!" *GA,* December 15, 1955. Harrell, *The Churches of Christ,* 40–44.

Chapter 7

1. Ernest R. Sandeen, *The Roots of Fundamentalism: British and American Millenarianism, 1800–1930* (Chicago: University of Chicago Press, 1970; Grand Rapids, MI: Baker Book House, 1978), 132–61 (1978 edition).

2. See William R. Glass, *Strangers in Zion: Fundamentalists in the South, 1900–1950* (Macon, GA: Mercer University Press, 2001) and B. Dwain Waldrep, "Lewis Sperry Chafer and the Development of Interdenominational Fundamentalism in the South, 1900–1950" (PhD diss., Auburn University, 2001).

3. Glass, *Strangers in Zion,* 37–39.

4. Walter R. Alexander, *All Out for God: The Challenging Career of John C. Cowell* (Chicago: Moody Press, 1911), 16–17, 25–26, 30–31, 56–73; John C. Cowell Jr., "The Moody Bible Institute," *Baptist Beacon* (Central Baptist Church), August 27, 1937; Gene Arnold Getz, "A History of Moody Bible Institute and Its Contributions to Evangelical Education" (PhD diss., New York University, 1967), 402.

5. Timothy P. Weber, *Living in the Shadow of the Second Coming: American Premillennialism 1875–1982* (Grand Rapids, MI: Academie Books, 1983), 238.

6. Lewis Sperry Chafer, "Early History of the Florida Bible Testimony Association," 1949, TMs, p. 1, Chafer Papers, Dallas Theological Seminary (hereafter cited as CPDTS).

7. Lewis Sperry Chafer, "Why a Denominational Unrelated Theological College?" Evangelical Theological College *Bulletin* 2 (February 1926): 3–4.

8. John A. Witmer, "'What Hath God Wrought'—Fifty Years of Dallas Theological Seminary," *Bibliotheca Sacra* 130 (October–December 1973): 297–98; Daniel G. Reid and others, eds., *Concise Dictionary of Christianity in America* (Downers Grove, IL: InterVarsity Press, 1995), s.v. "Chafer, Lewis Sperry," "Thomas, William Henry Griffith," and "Winchester, Alexander Brown."

9. Lewis Sperry Chafer, "Reaction to the 1942 National Conference for United Action Held at Saint Louis, Missouri," in *Evangelical Action: A Report of the Organization of the National Association of Evangelicals for United Action,* ed. Executive Committee (Boston: United Action Press, 1942), 144; Lewis Sperry Chafer, Dallas, to James Oliver Buswell Jr., Wheaton, Illinois, February 14, 1930; quoted in John. D. Hannah, "The Social and Intellectual History of the Origins of the Evangelical Theological College" (PhD diss., University of Texas at Dallas, 1959), 153.

10. John B. Boles, *The Great Revival: Beginnings of the Bible Belt* (Lexington: University Press of Kentucky, 1972).

11. Joel A. Carpenter, *Revive Us Again: The Reawakening of American Fundamentalism* (New York: Oxford University Press, 1997), 43; Joel A. Carpenter, "From Fundamentalism to the New Evangelical Coalition," in *Evangelicalism and Modern America,* ed. George Marsden (Grand Rapids, MI: Eerdmans Publishing, 1984), 4–5.

12. Christian Smith, *American Evangelicalism: Embattled and Thriving* (Chicago: University of Chicago Press, 1998), 9.

13. George Marsden, *Fundamentalism and American Culture: The Shaping of Twentieth-Century Evangelicalism* (New York: Oxford University Press, 1980), 179.

14. George Brown Tindall, *The Emergence of the New South, 1913–1945* (Baton Rouge: Louisiana State University Press, 1967), 7–8, 196–98.

15. Kenneth K. Bailey, *Southern White Protestantism in the Twentieth Century* (New York: Harper and Row, 1964), 16–17, 162–63.

16. Thomas McKinney, Memphis, to Local Pastors, Memphis, February 18, 1947, Archives, CPDTS.

17. Gene A. Getz, *MBI: The Story of Moody Bible Institute,* rev. ed. by James M. Vincent (Chicago: Moody Press, 1986), 65–67.

18. Lewis Sperry Chafer, "Workers Together with God," *Pioneer of a New Era* 10 (August 1931): 8.

19. Lewis Sperry Chafer, *Major Bible Themes* (Dallas: Dallas Theological Seminary, 1926; reprint, Grand Rapids, MI: Dunham Publications, 1964), vii–viii (page citations are to the reprint edition).

20. R. Lofton Hudson, "Modernistic Fundamentalism," *Baptist and Reflector,* October 19, 1944.

21. John L. Girardeau, "Address Delivered on Confederate Memorial Day at Charleston, South Carolina, on the Occasion of the Reinterment of the Carolina Dead from Gettysburg" (Charleston, SC: 1871), quoted in Ernest Trice Thompson, *Presbyterians in the South,* 3 vols., vol. 2, *1861–1890* (Richmond: John Knox Press, 1973), 2:14–15.

22. Samuel S. Hill, *The South and North in American Religion* (Athens: University of Georgia Press, 1980), 106.

23. Wayne Flynt, *Alabama Baptists: Southern Baptists in the Heart of Dixie* (Tuscaloosa: The University of Alabama Press, 1998), 251. See also Charles Reagan Wilson, *Baptized in Blood: The Religion of the Lost Cause, 1865–1920* (Athens: University of Georgia Press, 1980).

24. James E. Bear, "Dispensationalism and the Covenant of Grace," *Union Seminary Review* 49 (July 1938): 285–307.

25. Thompson, *Presbyterians in the South,* 3:488.

26. Ibid., 3:487; 558–66.

27. Albert Sidney Johnson, Charlotte, to Lewis Sperry Chafer, Dallas, February 13, 1939, Archives, CPDTS.

28. *Minutes,* North Alabama Presbytery, April 17, 1940, PCUSA Department of History, Montreat, North Carolina; *Minutes,* General Assembly of the Presbyterian Church in the United States, 1940, 83, PCUSA Department of History, Montreat, North Carolina (hereafter cited as *Minutes,* PCUS).

29. *Minutes,* PCUS, 1941, 60.

30. Lewis Sperry Chafer, Dallas, to Alexander H. Sauerwein, Huntington, New York, June 29, 1943, Archives, CPDTS.

31. *Minutes,* PCUS, 1943, 122.

32. *Minutes,* PCUS, 1943, 129.

33. *Minutes,* PCUS, 1944, 126.

34. Timothy George, "Southern Baptist Relationships with Other Protestants," *Baptist History and Heritage* 25 (July 1990): 28–29. See also R. Albert Mohler Jr., "The Southern Baptist Convention and the Issue of Interdenominational Relationships: A Memorandum Prepared for the Great Commission Council of the Southern Baptist Convention," *Fidelitas,* 6-12-00, http://web.archive.org/web/20020417182404/http://www.sbts.edu/mohler/fidelitas/sbcandecumenism.html, accessed August 29, 2011.

35. "Southern Baptist Concerned about Fundamentalist Invasion," *The Baptist,* October 7, 1922.

36. O. W. Taylor, "Postmillennial and Premillennial Ramming," *Baptist and Reflector,* May 12, 1949.

37. O. W. Taylor, "Essentials and Non-Essentials," *Baptist and Reflector,* May 9, 1940.

38. Duke K. McCall, "Northern Fundamentalism," *Baptist and Reflector,* September 3, 1953.

39. R. Lofton Hudson, "Modernistic Fundamentalism," *Baptist and Reflector,* October 19, 1944.

40. Ibid.

41. Russell Bradley Jones, "A Digest of Religious Thought," *Baptist and Reflector,* June 2, 1949.

42. Norris Gilliam, "Denominational Leadership Moulded by Our Baptist Schools," *Baptist and Reflector,* September 15, 1949.

43. "Denominational Integrity," *Baptist and Reflector,* March 27, 1952.

44. W. Ross Edwards, "That Unnamed Denomination," *Baptist and Reflector,* January 3, 1952; M. Theron Rankin, "Non-Denominationalism, Inter-Denominationalism, and the Church," *Baptist and Reflector,* January 8, 1953; William R. Rigell, "A Serious Situation," *Baptist and Reflector,* February 19, 1953.

45. T. C. Gardner, "Baptist Youth Sponsoring a Non-Denominational Convention," *Baptist and Reflector,* October 1, 1953.

46. "Report of the Committee on Relations with other Religious Bodies" (Houston, Texas, May 1953, typewritten), 3, Records of the Executive Committee, Southern Baptist Historical Library and Archives, Nashville, Tennessee.

47. Ibid.

48. Ibid.

49. Ibid., 4–5; T. C. Gardner, Dallas, to Porter Routh, Nashville, March 11, 1953, March 16, 1953, Records of the Executive Committee, Southern Baptist Historical Library and Archives, Nashville, Tennessee.

50. T. C. Gardner, Dallas, to Porter Routh, Nashville, July 24, 1953, Records of the Executive Committee, Southern Baptist Historical Library and Archives, Nashville, Tennessee.

51. "A Resume of Significant Events in the History of Bible Schools and Their Relationship to the SBC," typed manuscript, 1–2, Records of the Executive Committee, Southern Baptist Historical Library and Archives, Nashville, Tennessee; Gilbert L. Guffin, Birmingham, to A. H. Reid, Montgomery, February 24, 1947, Reid Papers, Special Collections, Samford University, Birmingham, Alabama; F. Wilbur Helmbold, *Born of the Needs of the People: The Extension Ministry of Samford University* (Birmingham: Banner Press, 1967), 15.

52. "Resume of Significant Events," 1–2; M. A. Huggins, Raleigh, to F. Russell Purdy, Lexington, July 2, 1953, Records of the Executive Committee, Southern Baptist Historical Library and Archives, Nashville, Tennessee.

53. Two Baptist Associations and one state convention established Bible institutes during the 1940s. The Baptist State Convention of North Carolina particularly had the interdenominational Bible institute movement in mind when it created Fruitland Baptist Bible Institute in 1946. The other schools were Florida Baptist Bible Institute established by the South Florida Association in 1943 and West Kentucky Baptist Bible Institute begun by the West Kentucky Baptist Association in 1945.

54. "Resume of Significant Events," 3–4; George C. Humphrey, "Education for Ministers," *Baptist and Reflector,* August 25, 1949.

55. F. Russell Purdy, Lexington, to State Secretaries, June 26, 1953; Charles F. Sims, Columbia, to F. Russell Purdy, Lexington, July 2, 1953; James R. Bryant, Richmond, to F. Russell Purdy, Lexington, July 2, 1953; J. Woodrow Fuller, Dallas, to F. Russell Purdy, Lexington, n.d.; Charles W. Pope, Nashville, to F. Russell Purdy, Lexington, July 1, 1953; Chester L. Quarles, Jackson, to F. Russell Purdy, Lexington, July 6, 1953; Floyd B. Chaffin, Alexandria, to F. Russell Purdy, Lexington, July 2, 1953; James W. Merritt, Atlanta, to F. Russell Purdy, Lexington, July 1, 1953; John Maguire, Jacksonville, to F. Russell Purdy, Lexington, July 3, 1953; B. L. Bridges, Little Rock, to F. Russell Purdy, Lexington, July 1, 1953; all located in Records of the Executive Committee, Southern Baptist Historical Library and Archives, Nashville, Tennessee.

56. "Resume of Significant Events," 5–6.

57. W. Wiley Richards, *Winds of Doctrines: The Origin and Development of Southern Baptist Theology* (Lanham, MD: University Press of America, 1991), 204–5.

58. Hannah, "Social and Intellectual History," 364–67.

59. For an in-depth study of the origins of one of these nondenominational churches, see B. Dwain Waldrep, "Lewis Sperry Chafer and the Roots of Nondenominational Fundamentalism in the South," *Journal of Southern History* 73 (November 2007): 807–36.

60. Ruth E. Mitchell, "History of the First Evangelical Church," undated typed manuscript, no pagination, located in the Women's Auxiliary Scrapbook at the First Evangelical Church, Memphis, Tennessee; *Sunday Bulletin,* Evangelical Community Church, March 8, 1936.

61. Waldrep, "Lewis Sperry Chafer and the Development of Interdenominational Fundamentalism in the South," 116–21.

62. See David Edwin Harrell Jr., ed., *Varieties of Southern Evangelicalism* (Macon, GA: Mercer University Press, 1981).

Conclusion

1. H. Richard Niebuhr, *The Social Sources of Denominationalism* (1929; Gloucester, MA: Peter Smith, 1987), 16.

2. David Edwin Harrell Jr., "Peculiar People: A Rationale for Modern Conservative Disciples," in *Disciples and the Church Universal,* ed. Robert O. Fife, David Edwin Harrell Jr., and Ronald E. Osborn (Nashville: Disciples of Christ Historical Society, 1967), 43.

3. Richard T. Hughes, ed., *The Primitive Church in the Modern World,* (Urbana: University of Illinois Press, 1995), 118.

4. Harrell, "Peculiar People," 43.

5. Richard T. Hughes, ed., *The American Quest for the Primitive Church* (Urbana: University of Illinois Press, 1988), 242.

6. Karl Barth, *Protestant Theology in the Nineteenth Century* (1947; Grand Rapids, MI: William B. Eerdmans Publishing, 2002), 8.

7. Hughes, *American Quest for the Primitive Church,* 244.

8. Richard T. Hughes, "David Edwin Harrell Jr. and the History of the Stone-Campbell Tradition," in this volume.

9. Harrell, "Peculiar People," 41.

10. Ibid., 43.

11. Ibid.

12. Ibid.

13. Ibid., 44.

Contributors

Scott Billingsley is Associate Professor of History and Director of the Graduate Social Studies Education Program at the University of North Carolina at Pembroke. He received his BA from David Lipscomb University, MA from Middle Tennessee State University, and PhD from Auburn University. He has taught at UNCP since 2003. His research focuses on the modern charismatic movement and the history of Disciples of Christ, Christian Churches, and Churches of Christ. His first book is titled *It's a New Day: Race and Gender in the Modern Charismatic Movement* (The University of Alabama Press, 2008), and he is currently working on a biography of Barton W. Stone.

Wayne Flynt is Distinguished University Professor Emeritus at Auburn University. Author of twelve books about southern poverty, politics, and religion, Flynt is a double Pulitzer Prize nominee, winner of the Lillian Smith prize for nonfiction, three-time awardee of the McMillan Prize for the best manuscript in Alabama history, and twice a winner of the Alabama Library Association prize for nonfiction. As an active advocate for the poor, Flynt has won many awards, including several from the University of Alabama: the Clarence Cason Award for writing and the Hugo Black Award for public service. In 1992 the *Mobile Press-Register* named Flynt its first "Alabamian of the Year." He was also elected to the Alabama Academy of Honor, a statewide organization honoring one hundred living Alabamians who have distinguished themselves in various endeavors.

James R. Goff Jr. is currently serving as Professor of History at Appalachian State University in Boone, North Carolina. He is the author of

Fields White unto Harvest: Charles F. Parham and the Missionary Origins of Pentecostalism (University of Arkansas Press, 1988) and *Close Harmony: A History of Southern Gospel* (University of North Carolina Press, 2002). He is also the coeditor of *Portraits of a Generation: Early Pentecostal Leaders* (University of Arkansas Press, 2002).

John C. Hardin is Special Projects Archivist at the Alabama Department of Archives and History in Montgomery. He received his PhD in history from Auburn University in 2009 and he holds a master's degree in biblical studies from Lipscomb University in Nashville, Tennessee. His research interests include the history of the American South, particularly Alabama, and the history of the Churches of Christ.

Samuel S. Hill received his PhD in religion from Duke University. He is Professor Emeritus in the Department of Religion at the University of Florida where he was department chair from 1972 to 1977. He has served as a faculty member at the University of North Carolina and Stetson University. In 1993 he was Visiting Eminent Scholar at Auburn University. His areas of special interest include religion in southern culture, religion in American culture, modern western religious movements, comparative study and history of western religion, politics and religion, and social ethics.

Richard T. Hughes is Distinguished Professor of Religion and Director of the Sider Institute for Anabaptist, Pietist, and Wesleyan Studies at Messiah College. The author or editor of seventeen books, Hughes's most recent work has focused on the intersection between religion and American nationalism in *Myths America Lives By* (University of Illinois Press, 2003) and *Christian America and the Kingdom of God* (University of Illinois Press, 2009). Like Professor Harrell, he has also written extensively on the history of the Churches of Christ, and his essay in this book assesses Harrell's work in that field.

Beth Barton Schweiger teaches early American social and cultural history at the University of Arkansas. She is the author of *The Gospel Working Up: Progress and the Pulpit in Nineteenth-Century Virginia* (Oxford University Press, 2000) and coeditor, with Donald G. Mathews, of *Religion in the American South: Protestants and Others in History and Culture* (University of North Carolina Press, 2004). She is completing *The Literate South: Reading and Freedom in the Early United States.*

Grant Wacker is Professor of Christian History and Director of the Graduate Program in Religion at Duke University. He was educated at Stanford University (BA) and Harvard University (PhD). He taught at the University of North Carolina from 1977 until he moved to Duke in 1992. An active United Methodist layman, his teaching and research interests fall in the areas of evangelical culture, pentecostal history, international missions, and mainline Protestant thought.

B. Dwain Waldrep earned his PhD at Auburn University and is Professor of History and Chair of the Department of Arts and Sciences at Southeastern Bible College in Birmingham, Alabama. He is the author of numerous encyclopedia and journal articles on Protestant fundamentalism in America.

Charles Reagan Wilson is the Kelly Gene Cook Sr. Chair of History and Professor of Southern Studies at the University of Mississippi, where he has taught since 1981. He received bachelor's and master's degrees from the University of Texas at El Paso and earned his PhD in history from the University of Texas at Austin. He is the author of *Baptized in Blood: The Religion of the Lost Cause, 1865–1920* (University of Georgia Press, 1980) and coeditor with Bill Ferris of the *Encyclopedia of Southern Culture* (University of North Carolina Press, 1989), which received the Dartmouth Prize from the American Library Association as the best reference book of the year.

Index